TRANSFORMING
CORPORATE
LEADERSHIP

TRANSFORMING CORPORATE LEADERSHIP

◆

PATRICK MILEHAM

and

KEITH SPACIE

London · Hong Kong · Johannesburg · Melbourne
Singapore · Washington DC

PITMAN PUBLISHING
128 Long Acre, London WC2E 9AN
Tel: +44 (0)171 447 2000
Fax: +44 (0)171 240 5771

A Division of Pearson Professional Limited

First published in Great Britain 1996

British Library Cataloguing in Publication Data
A CIP catalogue record for this book can be obtained
from the British Library.

ISBN 0 273 61457 6

1 3 5 7 9 10 8 6 4 2

Typeset by Northern Phototypesetting Co Ltd, Bolton
Printed and bound in Great Britain by
Biddles Ltd, Guildford and King's Lynn

*The Publishers' policy is to use paper manufactured
from sustainable forests.*

About the Authors

PATRICK MILEHAM spent 28 years until 1992 in a number of different functional posts in the regular Army, most of which involved leading and/or training others in leadership skills. In the latter part of his career, he devised and developed a number of innovative schemes of leadership training.

A graduate of Cambridge, he holds a post at the University of Paisley and is associate lecturer in the Centre for Leadership Studies, University of Surrey. He is active as a coach and academic consultant and produced in 1995 a large scale study of boardroom leadership and corporate governance, published by the Institute of Management and Centre for Leadership Studies. He has written a number of books and numerous articles on a diversity of subjects, including corporate ethics.

KEITH SPACIE CB OBE, has been involved actively in the leadership field for much of the past 40 years – as practitioner, follower, coach and researcher.

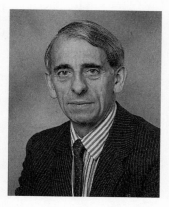

He served his apprenticeship as a leader in the jungles of Malaya, learning to lead the hard way at the age of 20 in charge of a group of 40 sometimes reluctant conscripts. For the next 30 years he practiced, experienced and observed both good and bad leadership in a wide variety of circumstances and at different levels, culminating in a period in 1983–4 as the Military Commissioner in the Falkland Islands. He also spent a period developing young leaders at Sandhurst. For the past eight-and-a-half years he has been involved in studying, researching, coaching and advising on leadership and teamworking in both private and public sectors, both with his own consultancy firm and at the University of Surrey, where he established the Centre for Leadership Studies.

Leadership and management; management and leadership: for success, the two go together. The one without the other is diminished if not negated altogether. Leadership is of the spirit, its practice and art; management is a science, it is all to do with the ordering of resources, of things material. The two together, properly done: unstoppable!

In this book you will find a fine analysis of and a deep insight into the art of leadership that cannot but help you improve your performance in the running of your business, enterprise or organization. It will help you to understand why this is so, and how you may join that multitude of people who, down through the ages, have had a positive hand in the direction of human endeavour. It is a book not merely for reading once only. For those of us in positions of influence, the performance checks set out in its pages should be a ready, handy manual, a constant reminder of what we should be about. Every leader can improve, can do better.

If our humanity is to survive, if we are to be successful in confronting the problems that face us, leadership of the very highest order is going to be needed.

Sir Richard Trant
Chairman, Hunting Engineering, Defence Division

CONTENTS

◆

Part II
THE LEADERSHIP FIELD

Part III
LEADING MORE EFFECTIVELY

Part IV
TRANSFORMING FOR THE MILLENNIUM

PREFACE

◆

One of the quotations in this book, which is a veritable mine of useful quotations, ideas and advice, is by that brilliant War-time leader, Field Marshal Slim: "There is nobody who cannot vastly improve his powers of leadership by a little thought and practice." That thought is justification for this book, for it knocks on the head the rather daft notion that leaders are born not made and that, therefore, there is little point in striving to improve one's quality of leadership. Even if leadership cannot be taught it can certainly be improved and, because it invariably makes the difference between success and failure in any enterprise, Patrick Mileham and Keith Spacie decided to write what amounts to a practitioner's guide to leadership.

For the same reason Philippe de Backer, Charles Farkas and I recently wrote and published *Maximum Leadership*. Our hypothesis was that if we interviewed the world's top business leaders (and we spoke to 160 of them) and asked them how they added value to their businesses, the nature of business leadership in its different forms would emerge and provide lessons which would be useful to people running companies or aspiring to do so.

The two books complement each other and together give an excellent guide to those involved or planning to be involved at all levels in the running of businesses and other enterprises. The gap between success and failure is frighteningly small – hopefully these practical starters on leadership will help to improve the odds in favour of success.

Allan Sheppard

FOREWORD

◆

The Book

The book is written in a style and format designed for easy reading and reference. As far as is practicable it steers clear of academic abstraction, and we have tried to avoid the use of jargon and platitudes. It is above all designed to give practical help and guidance – we have had many years of practical experience in the field of leadership and in helping others develop their effectiveness as leaders – hoping that at the same time it will serve to stimulate thinking.

Our hope is that the book will contribute to both individual and corporate development, and be used as either a rapid read by a busy senior executive, a reference book, or a basis for discussion and study in business and corporate development programs. Our belief is that its greatest value will be to those who already have a basis of practical experience and with people.

We have no doubt that some will take positive issue with what we have written. To others, we may not have argued our case in some instances fully or convincingly. Accepting that it is seldom ever possible to produce a completely "finished" book on a topic such as we have chosen, we are willing always to develop our thoughts with others, or where appropriate to give advice.

The Authors

Keith Spacie: Although I have been involved in the practical side of leadership for most of my life, I did not begin to think about it in a structured way until some eight or nine years ago. Up to that point I had pursued my career by trying to put into practice what I had learned through observation and experience. And as is so often the case, bad experiences taught me more than the good – the effects of bad or indifferent leadership usually being easier to identify and quantify. As is also often the case, I had remarkably little by way of effective leadership coaching en route, although I did enjoy the benefits of a comprehensive general development program. I was in turn guilty of not putting sufficient emphasis myself on the coaching of others. *Mea culpa*.

Following a change of careers, I became involved more deeply in the training and development field. What surprised me was how little people generally understood about leadership, which was just beginning to be recognized as a vitally important but neglected area of human activity, and what being an effective leader involved. The situation was not helped by individuals and organizations setting themselves up as leadership experts with neither the practical experience nor the academic background to fulfill such a role. They were relying in the main on knowledge or ideas gleaned from books, often imported, and using theories and jargon that were offputting, to say the least. Moreover, they were promoting leadership as a completely novel process, and in a way that did not always relate to the real world. Too often the means they used became ends in themselves. Surprisingly, I found that very little research had been or was being done in this field in the UK – certainly not on a multi-disciplinary basis – and leadership is an activity that touches on a number of disciplines.

Against that background, I have tried to put down my thoughts and ideas on leadership in a way with which people involved in the practice of leadership can readily identify. I have not set out to produce a model and say this is how to do it. Rather, I have tried to help people understand a little better the concept of leadership, to stimulate thinking about this all-important area, and most importantly to suggest ways in which leaders might improve their performance.

Patrick Mileham: My career also took me into the mêlée of intense practical activity. My instinct was to ponder what was beyond the immediate activities, and the observable personal interrelationships of those around me. It became clear that many questions just cannot be fully answered: one has to work hard at the job alongside others and plan how to make continuous improvement and growth – in people and organizational performance.

Even in the best organized occupations, one sees people who are competent and effective and those who are not; those who are easy to get on with (whether subordinates, colleagues or superiors) and those who are difficult. We ourselves react to them according to our temperament and judgment. They will judge us and react too. If only everyone else was consistently competent and always easy to get on with; ditto ourselves!

In mid-career I unexpectedly discovered considerable leadership potential in an identifiable group, within a large organization in which I worked. For reasons of organizational culture, individuals were being overlooked for career advancement. They and the organization deserved better. I set about devising a scheme of action and a coaching regime, which transformed most of them and their career prospects, including some who quickly achieved spectacular success. It is very satisfying to observe the achievements of those one has helped; recognition for oneself is incidental.

In more recent years I have discovered that the dual role of participant–observer is a vital skill for those at the top of organizations to acquire. It is not enough for a board member or senior executive to be clever, far sighted and proactive. If he or she is unaware both of other people's motivation and the action/reaction/interaction between people at all levels, that director or executive will be less effective a leader than they could be – sometimes much less. Apart from those rare, natural born and brilliant leaders, most of us need to be healthily self-critical, learn from our experience and acquire along the way guidance as to the questions to be asked. Those are the aims of the book.

We acknowledge the part that numerous people played in formulating our ideas over many years, wittingly and unwittingly. In the past year we have interviewed a number of leaders, specifically for their comments on particular topics for inclusion in the book. We are grateful for their assistance.

We thank Richard Stagg and Sally Green, our editors at Pitman Publishing, an impressive publishing house. Pat Stevenson spent many hours typing up innumerable drafts and we thank her for her cheerfulness and dedication.

Part I

◆

THE NEED FOR LEADERS

> ◆
>
> **Leadership begins and ends with human beings – their aspirations, emotions and motivation.**
>
> ◆

Chapter 1

◆

WHY LEADERSHIP?

A MULTIPLICITY OF MODELS

The resurgence of interest in leadership and leader performance, has been accompanied, especially in the USA, by a plethora of books seeking to promote formulae for success in this field. A number of the books, which in some instances have featured on bestseller lists both in the USA and elsewhere, have earned their charismatic authors cult status, as well as making them a great deal of money. Some of the examples used as models are impressive, although a number have subsequently failed. But for all their dynamic prescriptions, the questions remaining are nearly always: how valid are they in the round and do they have a universal applicability?

Popular formulae apart, there has also been a great deal of serious research into leadership over the past few decades, again centered mainly in the USA. This research has been conducted primarily by university-based behavioral scientists, starting with the Ohio State University and University of Michigan in the 1950s, seeking to determine among other things successful leader behavior patterns, as opposed to the innate qualities of leaders. The outcome has been a multiplicity of models and theories with titles such as "transactional," "transformational," "situational," "participative," "power-influence," "charismatic" and "principle-centered leadership," the main ones of which are summarized in the Appendix to this book. Undoubtedly, most if

3

not all have contributed to the general understanding of the subject, but on the whole the models and theories advanced are little known generally outside the USA, and in any case tend not to attract European readers.

UK practitioners particularly have an aversion to abstract theory, especially if this is wrapped up in unattractive jargon. They tend to follow approaches that are more practical, and their preference is for simple and flexible models, with considerable reliance on intuition. This may be a strength, and it may be a weakness. Perhaps it explains the relative popularity of the "action centered" model advocated by John Adair, the "team role" types identified by Meredith Belbin and the dynamic "hands-on" style of Sir John Harvey-Jones, as illustrated in his books and TV programs.

Arguably leadership is best observed and practised from a number of different viewpoints, if the practitioner is to gain the necessary multidimensional understanding of leadership.

It is our opinion that no one has yet developed a single model on theory with universal applicability, nor probably is anyone ever likely to. Arguably leadership is best observed and practiced from a number of different viewpoints, if the practitioner is to gain the necessary multidimensional un-derstanding of leadership.

In fact, implementing of any theory, plan, scheme or cultural process, is usually extremely difficult. Our point is that a very large part of any understanding about leadership is to do with the act of translating into practice philosophical, theoretical and practical insights, formulas and methods which have been investigated and proved. Leadership must be grounded in practical

Leadership must be grounded in practical activity.

4

activity: it cannot only be a theoretical concept any more than "health" can have any meaning without being linked to a living organism.

Some people do of course lead effectively without having or consciously following any particular theory, or adopting a specific approach. Accepting this, we believe that their effectiveness can be enhanced by a better understanding of some of the underlying theory, but particularly by measuring their own performance against what might be described as best practice. Furthermore we believe that while some core aspects of leadership are constant, every generation must learn in its own way about leading its own people. Some lessons can be passed on because generations overlap, but they need to be revalidated under new circumstances by the new leaders.

> **Every generation must learn in its own way about leading its own people.**

LEADERSHIP, LEADERS, LEADING

A principal reason why many discussions on leadership or leaders become confused is a failure to make a distinction between:

- the idea or concept of **leadership**, what it is;
- the desired characteristics of effective **leaders**, what we expect them to be and the skills and attributes we expect them to have;
- and **leading**, the successful practice of leadership, what we expect leaders to do.

The three are categorically of the same order and closely related, but at the same time need to be differentiated. We shall try to use "leader" and "leading" as much as possible, while reserving the more abstract word "leadership" for places where the two are combined for brevity (i.e. when a leader is leading).

One is also faced with very conflicting attitudes such as:

- those who see leadership as an unchanging process, something you can as it were take off the shelf and apply to any situation;
- those who see leadership in terms only of personal qualities (and often further argue that a person either has or has not the requisite qualities);
- those who see leadership merely as the application of a set of skills;
- those who see leadership as an exciting field of discovery and in it seek something revolutionary or new.

These attitudes obviously have a marked effect when it comes to the selection and development of leaders as well as the practice of leadership.

In reality some aspects of leadership are unchanging – such as the nature of leadership. Others are dynamic – depending on the conditions under which it is practiced. And the successful leader possesses both qualities and skills.

"The elements of leadership are constant although changed conditions may require a different technique."
Field Marshal Earl Wavell

GENERALISTS OR SPECIALISTS

Too often in our opinion leadership is regarded as a specialist field of its own, for the attention of a few people only. This idea is reinforced by the way it is sometimes presented. We reject this approach and take firmly the opposite view: that leadership is a "generalist skill" and that a majority of people have the capacity to practice it successfully, given guidance.

Specialists and generalists

In the managerial sense "specialists" are those whose job demands expert knowledge and competence, involving "deep analysis and concentration on a highly differentiated type of task or technology. To do things narrowly is a crucial part of doing them well."[1]

Generalist skills on the other hand are those required to integrate the specialist skills and knowledge of others – "to co-ordinate across a span of functions, tasks and specialisations." In terms of personality, generalists "relate to power, achievement, ambition, emotional stability, optimism, intelligence, analytical ability, intuition, a personable style and an ability to relate easily to a broad set of business specialists."[2]

Some it is true have what is described as a natural gift for leading which they exercise easily, and successfully, often in more than one context. Most of us, however, need some guidance to enable us to improve our understanding of leadership and perform effectively as leaders.

If we are honest, we probably need more guidance than we would admit to, and we can never stop learning.

If we are honest, we probably need more guidance than we would admit to, and we can never stop learning.

"There is nobody who cannot vastly improve his powers of leadership by a little thought and practice."

Field Marshal Viscount Slim

We are convinced that most people have ideas about what they are looking for, when some sort of leadership activity is necessary, or the concept is being considered in an abstract way. They

7

know "why" firm leadership is necessary. Yet analysis of "how" to implement good leadership practice – in individual actions or throughout the organization – frequently eludes them. Words describing the experience afterwards so often seem inadequate. We know the predicament well.

To end this first chapter we must emphasize that leadership begins and ends with human beings – their aspirations, emotions and motivation. At its highest level, how leaders lead can be associated with the very essence of humanity and the human spirit.

> **We must emphasize that leadership begins and ends with human beings – their aspirations, emotions and motivation.**

"Leadership is first and foremost ... human personality at its best. Leadership is the deepest revelation of the image of man. ... Leadership is the highest form of power; a loyalty to spiritual reality so that the leader can command the loyalty of others unto himself. ... Leadership is creative insight into the nature of our time. Leadership is prophecy, for it is vision of the best we can achieve."

Dr G. G. Kullmann (1931)[3]

Chapter 2

◆

THE LEADERSHIP VACUUM

A REDISCOVERY

A few years ago we undertook some research among chief executives and chairmen of large companies seeking to find out what their views were on strategic leadership. We discovered that few really saw themselves as leaders and seemed uncomfortable even using the word in relation to themselves. Perhaps they associated it in their minds with militarism and authoritarianism (they were mostly of an age to have done national service). More likely, it was a preoccupation with asset management, an overattention to the bottom line, and an outlook that was essentially short-term. Some did not even mention or seem to give much attention to people – in most cases their most important and valuable asset, the human capital that can bring the highest return of all, but only if properly led. They not only did not use the word or see themselves as a leader, but clearly did not practice being one either: we noticed that many of the same companies whose executives did not mention leadership and people suffered very rapidly during the recent recession.

But things have changed, and leadership is now back in fashion, or at least the word is. This is particularly true at national level, with seemingly endless debate in the media in many countries about political leadership: is he or is he not a leader; can his leadership transform the party and the nation, etc.? In this context leadership is clearly separated from any talk of management and economic factors. In industry too, or certainly in the more successful companies, there is in-creasing use of the word "leader" and its associated term "team leading," and the demise of such words as "charge-hand,"

> **But things have changed, and leadership is now back in fashion, or at least the word is.**

"progress chaser" and "supervisor". There is frequent talk of boardroom teams and institutional leaders.

Like many fashions, particularly in the world of business and organizations, the rediscovery of leadership – for that is essentially what it is – has been accompanied by new theorizing, a spate of new jargon, dogmatism and distortion. There has been renewed search for the holy grail of leadership, the indiscriminate and distorted use of words such as "vision" and "empowerment," and ridiculous claims that leadership should now replace management – claims which are as facile as those that hold leadership to be management by another name. Nevertheless, leadership's return is to be welcomed both for its own sake, because it can be turned to real effect in good leadership practice, and in a commercial sense it can have a marked affect on that bottom line which so excites board members and shareholders. Leadership is profit related.

> **Leadership is profit related.**
> **But what is this thing "leadership"?**

CONFUSION OF MEANINGS

But what is this thing "leadership"? Understanding what it is or what it entails causes problems for many people; as the American writer, Warren Bennis, has put it: "Leadership is the most observed and least understood phenomenon on earth." People's ideas and concepts of leadership vary enormously. To some it is a question of position or "being in charge." To others it is about style or sanction.

Leadership is about:

"the successful resolution of problems."
Dean Acheson

"persuading people to do what they should have done in the first place."
attributed to Harry Truman

"reason and calm judgement."
Tacitus

"dealing in hope."
Napoleon

"getting extraordinary performance out of ordinary people."
Sir John Harvey-Jones

At its most fundamental leadership is about people and about influencing others and giving them direction. Implicit is the idea of identifying the way ahead, and a following by others. It is also about helping others to cope with the changes, uncertainties

At its most fundamental leadership is about people and about influencing others and giving them direction.

11

and risks that lie in their path. It can be attributed to groups as well as to individuals, as is the case in governments and boardrooms.

> **"Leadership:** *the position of a group of people leading or influencing others within a given context; the group itself; the action or influence necessary for the direction of effort in a group undertaking."*
>
> *Oxford English Dictionary*

All organizations are reliant on the willpower of their people – at all levels – more so than is generally appreciated. Too often, however, those managing organizations think of people only in a relatively abstract way, as just another resource like finance and materials – encouraged perhaps by the increasing use of the term "human resource." Yet the truth is that regardless of size or activity organizations depend to a large extent for their success on the interaction of people, their emotions, energies and potential to achieve a high level of performance – reliance thus on a far more variable resource than any other, variable as is human nature.

Regardless of size or activity organizations depend to a large extent for their success on the interaction of people, their emotions, energies and potential to achieve a high level of performance.

Importance of people

In some recent research, the question was "what explains the financial success of 40 major manufacturing firms over a 5-year span?" The five predictors were:

- market share;

- capital intensive and with greater technological advantage;

- size of assets of the firm;

- return on investment;

- emphasis on management of human resources.

"The last mentioned was three times more powerful than all the other factors combined."[4]

G. Hudson, University of Michigan Business School

Human resource management is, however, only the beginning. If people are led well the **leadership** factor will make even more of a difference.

LEADERSHIP AND MANAGEMENT

There is often considerable misunderstanding about the relationship between leadership and management. In the past decades we have seen the growth of management as an applied science and with it an emphasis on system and resource control. While this development is largely to be welcomed, management as a subject area has at the same time tended to subsume leadership as a specific function – to the extent that in many people's

> **There is often considerable misunder-standing about the relationship between leadership and management.**

minds the two have become synonymous. This has certainly been the case in some of the business schools. Even in the military sphere, the sector usually associated most closely with

13

leadership, the word "management" has been frequently used when what is meant is leadership.

A consequence of the growth of this more scientific approach to management has been the neglect of leadership as a social process and a disregard for the full importance of people. It led in many instances to a recognizable leadership void or vacuum – which has often been filled by strong "unofficial" leadership, for example of the trade unions. (Ironically perhaps, we never ceased referring to senior trade unionists as leaders.) Such a vacuum still exists in many organizations. And the existence of such a vacuum emphasizes that there is a discrete process called leadership.

Leadership vacuums

In the commercial field, the car industry in the 1960 and 1970s provides a graphic example of a leadership vacuum. In many companies management abrogated leadership almost entirely surrendering their leadership authority to the shopfloor union officials who determined by and large how the company operated, especially at the lower levels. The unions became a main medium for communication, a major force in decision-making, and the focus of loyalty – because managers were unwilling and felt incapable of playing their vital leadership role. Peter Sellers, in the film *I'm all Right, Jack*, parodied the situation well.

There are innumerable examples of leadership vacuums in the international and political fields and the dire consequences to which they can lead. The failure of the Weimar Republic and the consequent rise of Hitler is one such instance. Another is the League of Nations: The League of Nations was set up in World War I to maintain peace and secure the territorial inviolability and political independence of all states. Unfortunately the League was weakened by the absence of the USA and other major states. But in the 1930s certain powers defied the League with impunity. Japan invaded Manchuria in 1932 and Mussolini invaded Abyssinia in 1935 without effective sanctions. In 1935 Hitler introduced conscription thereby breaking clauses in the Treaty of Versailles. France appealed to the League but neither she nor Britain, the strongest powers in the League, were prepared to act. Public confidence in the League was lost and Hitler took advantage of the Abyssinia crisis to re-occupy the Rhineland with only a formal protest from France and Britain. Had France and Britain shown positive leadership and acted with strength of purpose at this stage, Hitler's bluff would have been called as the German generals thought that the weak, half trained German army was unequal to the task. Hitler and Mussolini signed a pact followed soon after by an agreement with the Japanese.

More recently in Bosnia we witnessed for at least two years a leadership vacuum. There was no practical leadership shown by the UN authorities and its constituent governments. Policy leadership was in effect surrendered to the media.

In most instances there is or needs to be a relationship between management and leadership. Leadership can of course exist in isolation and may not be associated with any management–administrative function. Intellectual leadership is one such example. It is also arguable that a

It is also arguable that a person can be an 'effective' leader yet be totally inadequate in a managerial sense. The reverse however is seldom true.

person can be an "effective" leader yet be totally inadequate in a managerial sense. The reverse however is seldom true. In practice most positions involving executive responsibility require

15

both leadership and management, the ratio depending on the nature of the task. Some tasks or jobs demand more in the way of leadership, in others there is a greater need for management and administrative skills. Expertise in what are essentially complementary areas does not have to be vested in the same person – although perhaps ideally it should be. In some circumstances they are provided effectively by two or more persons acting in harmony and in an interdependent way. There are good examples of this working successfully in a number of commercial undertakings.

Leadership duo No. 1

John is the ultimate shadowy backroom figure. He is brilliant with figures and money, and with redesigning structures. He is also very efficient. Without him the company would undoubtedly go under. But he is hopeless with people. Jenny is almost the exact opposite. She is not particularly well organized as a person and while understanding finance generally quickly loses interest in the details of the balance sheet. Yet she has a clear idea of where she is going, is excellent at selling the future to the staff and in motivating them to give of their best. Separately, they would probably fail. Together they are brilliant.

Leadership duo No. 2

"I followed the fortunes of three financial service companies with famous names, set up by a remarkable leader. This chairman knew exactly what the market wanted and was supremely competent in providing the products needed. He knew, however, that he was not good at leading people in the ordinary sense. He deliberately chose as his Chief Executive a brilliant 'people man' who was.

> *(The CEO could even sack someone and make them feel he was doing them a service.) As a leadership duo they complemented one another and placed the companies' performance consistently near the top of the league. Between them they were enormously successful. **Knowing your weaknesses is part of good leadership.**"*
>
> **Knowing your weaknesses is part of good leadership.**
>
> **Executive Personal Assistant**

The actual relationship between leadership and management has been debated widely and no doubt will continue to exercise academics:

- Some will argue that the two are essentially the same or inseparable.
- Others view them as totally separate functions.
- A third view is that they are discrete but related processes.
- Many, particularly in the USA, see management as being a part of leadership.
- Finally, there is the view that leadership has been subsumed by management.

To some extent the view of the relationship stems from an individual's definition of the functions. A growing consensus however appears to be that the two are discrete, but related. As Professor John Kotter of the Harvard Business School puts it: "Management complements leadership; it doesn't replace it." We would go further: management is complemented and enhanced by leadership.

Management is complemented and enhanced by leadership.

17

To help separate the two functions a worthwhile exercise is to list under each words that are used in various descriptions. Some that we have identified are:

Management	Leadership
• Science	• Art
• Objective	• Subjective
• Head	• Heart
• Efficiency	• Effectiveness
• Present	• Future
• Order	• Change
• Security	• Risk
• Planning	• Sets direction

Professor John Kotter of the Harvard Business School contrasts them thus:[5]

Management	Leadership
• Planning and budgeting	• Establishing direction
• Organizing and staffing	• Aligning people
• Controlling and problem-solving	• Monitoring and improving
• Producing a degree of predictability and order	• Producing change

Although both exercises seek to emphasize the distinction, in reality there is often a blurring of edges between the two functions.

LEADERSHIP AND MANAGEMENT – THE LINK

Unfortunately, we seem to lack a suitable or acceptable word in the English language to describe adequately the coming together of leadership and management in an organizational sense. The military and police use the word "command," which would not generally be acceptable elsewhere (although at least one large retailing company refers to "command of a store"). Some writers have introduced the term leader-manager, or manager-leader, to describe the individual, but many find this clumsy and ambiguous. In a corporate sense the word "governance" is now used increasingly, although arguably the word has unfortunate connotations of stuffiness, and is unlikely to be acceptable other than in large organizations or institutions. The word "direction" is sometimes used although it seems this might be too lofty and prescriptive. Unfortunately perhaps and depending on the user's bias people are more likely to use either management or leadership to cover both functions.

> **Unfortunately, we seem to lack a suitable or acceptable word in the English language to describe adequately the coming together of leadership and management in a non-organizational sense.**

LEADERSHIP AND POWER

Winston Churchill once described leadership as "the intelligent use of power," although he did not define what he meant by power. The interpretation and reconciliation of this relationship causes difficulty to some, who see power purely in terms of material strength or of sanction and perhaps seek to acquire and exert it in those terms. If there is overmuch concentration of power in too few hands without counterbalances, power may corrupt and become self-defeating. Overmuch diffusion of power can be enervating and lead to paralysis or anarchy – whether in politics, public institutions or commerce. Either way leadership suffers.

> **Winston Churchill once described leadership as "the intelligent use of power."**

How organizations balance power with organizational aims is often a matter of huge debate, intense disagreement and constant attempts to effect a shift of power to satisfy a particular partisan goal.

Yet there are many instances when leadership has to be exercised without any direct power backing. Effective democratic leadership is far more difficult to achieve and maintain than authoritarian leadership. Consider the plc nonexecutive chairman or director, the church leader, or increasingly the school teacher and those responsible in the National Health Service. They have to rely obviously on those less readily tangible sources of power – personality, strength of character, persuasiveness and moral argument. If successful, the outcome is usually far more effective and longer lasting.

Chapter 3

♦

LEADERS

*"**Leader**: a person who by force of example, talents or qualities of leadership plays a directing role, wields commanding influence, or has a following in any sphere of activity or thought."*

Chambers Dictionary

THE POSITION OF THE LEADER

The leader is a recognized individual within a group which has an identifiable purpose. Some individuals are appointed to a position of leadership with or without designated authority, responsibilities and powers of sanction. These individuals may or may not turn out to be effective leaders, or be recognized as leaders by the group. In other situations a leader emerges informally

The leader is a recognized individual within a group which has an identifiable purpose

and is accepted as such by those in the group. Either way, to be effective he or she has to fulfill the leadership expectations of those who follow. The leader's position is best found in the hearts and minds of the followers.

21

WHAT ARE WE LOOKING FOR?

For many years, indeed until relatively recently, the tendency was to look at leaders in terms of what were perceived to be their innate qualities. It was a failure to reach agreement on what those innate qualities are that led scientists and academics in the 1940s onwards to start looking at leaders in a different way, focusing on practice and behavior rather than personality, and on the normal person rather than the exceptional. But personality and personality traits cannot be disregarded entirely. Indeed, today we see a renewed search by some writers for qualities that are deemed to be essential.

LEADERS HAVE?

Some of the suggested qualities of leaders are:

Ambition	*Faith*	*Outgoing*
Cheerfulness	*Fairness*	*Personality*
Commonsense	*Flexibility*	*Resilience*
Cooperation	*Foresight*	*Self-control*
Courage	*Humor*	*Sensitivity*
Dedication	*Initiative*	*Sympathy*
Dependability	*Integrity*	*Tact*
Determination	*Intellect*	*Trust*
Drive	*Intuition*	*Tenacity*
Endurance	*Judgment*	*Toughness*
Energy	*Knowledge*	*Uncommon sense*
Enthusiasm	*Loyalty*	*Willpower*

This list, however, begs the questions:

- Do you have to have all the qualities?
- Which are the most important?

- How do you measure them?
- What value can you give to each?
- Can you be an effective leader lacking those regarded as the most important?
- How do you develop such qualities as humor, commonsense, etc?

Which do you, the reader, place in your top three or top six? The qualities approach has its merits, and can assist in the selection and appraisal of leaders.

LEADERS NEED?

If a more comprehensive approach is taken, experience, observation and analysis suggest that effective leaders possess a number of personal attributes which might be viewed as fundamental, especially within the context of a democratic society. It is suggested that some agreement on these fundamentals is essential in any organization both for purposes of selection and to serve as a benchmark for individual development and leadership practice.

Some of these fundamentals are likely to be personal qualities – although the debate on what are the key qualities is an endless one, as is discussion on their relative values, measurement, and the extent to which they are innate or can be developed; some are traits or developable skills.

Personal integrity

Personal integrity is the quality that appears more frequently on lists of desirable attributes than perhaps any other. The need for integrity has been highlighted by a number of well-publicized incidents in recent years in both public and private sectors, in sport as well as in commercial and professional life. In this sense integrity encompasses honesty, moral behavior and ethical values or principles.

> **"Integrity:** *Condition of uncorruptedness, soundness, unimpaired moral state, freedom from moral corruption, soundness of moral principle, honesty ... fair dealing."*
>
> Oxford English Dictionary
>
> **Ethics:** *"the difference between morality and ethics is easy to remember if one speaks of moral standards of* **behaviour** *and ethical systems of* **belief."**[6]

Other than in the most trivial circumstances, any behavior, or conduct of business between persons has a moral content. A good leader, assumes a strong moral responsibility towards those he or she leads. It is moral authority above all which differentiates his position from that of symbolic status, rank or other formal legitimacy.

Integrity has another and highly significant meaning, that is the binding together of a group or team; the opposite of disintegration. Moral integrity and group integrity are closely linked, and we shall discuss this in detail later.

It is comparatively easy to behave in a morally upright and

When the pressure is on, either in a competitive or material sense, it can be difficult to resist cutting moral corners – and tempting to reject the need for integrity or moral values entirely.

principled way according to established standards, when things are normal. But when the pressure is on, either in a competitive or material sense, it can be difficult to resist cutting moral corners – and tempting to reject the need for integrity or moral values entirely.

24

Cutting moral corners: 1

There have been a number of well-publicized cases in recent years of senior executives of companies and institutions being accused and convicted of "cutting moral corners" or worse to hide either their own shortcomings or failures, or through sheer personal greed. They have been related in the main to financial dealings involving depositors' or investors' money, pension funds and share dealings. They have inflicted severe damage to public confidence in commercial leadership as well as to the institutions and companies themselves and to the City and its regulation. It has also led to even more regulatory legislation to protect the public.

Any group, team or organization takes its moral tone and value system from its leader, from his or her example, or what is said, and from what is condemned or condoned. It is not something that can be easily measured or quantified. It is something that is felt by the team or organization, and expressed in its performance and outlook.

The threat of being found out or censored imposes a degree of "integrity control." There are many occasions however when that likelihood is perceived to be less, and in these circumstances, especially when the pressure is on, the temptations to take a short cut can be strong.

Cutting moral corners: 2

Much prominence has been given to shortcomings in major police investigations. There is great public and political pressure on the police to obtain convictions in high-profile cases. This has resulted in cases of wrongful imprisonment – sometimes for years – before convictions have been overturned. The Guildford bomb case was one such.

Willingness to accept responsibility

Closely linked to personal integrity is a willingness to accept responsibility for decisions made and happenings within one's area of responsibility. President Truman is reputed to have had a sign on his desk saying: "The buck stops here." The same adage could be applied to anyone in a leadership position. There was a time when a government minister would resign if the performance of his or her department was seen to be less than adequate. Lord Carrington as Foreign Secretary is one who saw that the Falklands conflict was a result of diplomatic mistakes and resigned immediately. More recently ministers have shown a remarkable reluctance to follow the high-principled resignation tradition. They seem to have concentrated their minds | **The buck stops here.** more on excuses and scapegoats, than ever they did on the principle of responsibility or, more generally, in making the best decisions in the public's interest. It is notable too that few company directors ever resign when things for which they are responsible go wrong – unless they are paid exorbitant compensation to help them on their way, rather than be sacked by the shareholders meeting.

Understanding people

Leadership is about people. Of fundamental importance to a leader therefore is an understanding of people, their needs, what motivates them, how they think and how they react and furthermore, how they react as groups. What is surprising is how seldom an interest in and understanding of people is a factor to be considered when selecting some-

Leadership is about people.

one for an appointment that requires leadership. Yet for most companies these days people are the most expensive resource. It begs the question: would you appoint someone to the same position who had no understanding of or interest in the financial side?

> *"Many American companies are in trouble, and I believe an important contributing factor has been the neglect of the human element in business."*
>
> **Donald Peterson (former CEO of the Ford Motor Co)**
> **and John Hillkirk in *Teamwork***

In an hour-long discussion with the chairman of a major engineering and manufacturing company on the subject of "strategic leadership", people were not mentioned even once. Yet the root cause of all the company's troubles – which were considerable – were clearly people related.

Whether it is essential for an effective leader positively to like people – constantly surrounded by people, working, talking and living with people, day in day out – is a difficult question to answer. Those asking the question have in mind certain prominent leaders who reputedly had little time for those they led. Historical analysis is not very helpful either way. The important conclusion is that such leaders probably had a good understanding of people. The really effective leaders, set against the

27

absolute judgment of history, were those who used people's talents and enthusiasms to achieve great and worthy objectives. Those who were perceived merely to have manipulated people are remembered for that and their work is so judged.

Communication

It has been said that communication oils the wheels of leadership. Undoubtedly, good communication is essential for leadership to be effective. Many pay lip service to its importance, but the reality is that communication in most organizations is poor. Some are reluctant to share information; either it is seen as a source of power, or there is a lack of trust. The reality is that if people are not informed they will guess – with a 50 per cent chance that they will guess wrongly, or give of less than their best.

Effective leaders listen, and make use of information and ideas from others as well as imparting it.

Communication is of course a two-way process. Effective leaders listen, and make use of information and ideas from others as well as imparting it. The need is also multidirectional: inwards, outwards, upwards, downwards and sideways.

"Dennis Specialist Vehicles, attribute their market success after their management buy out to their emphasis on leadership and communication ... regularly programmed communication that underpins the leadership."

Consultants' Report

Selflessness

Selflessness, together with the setting of example, is agreed by many to be a trait without which leaders cannot hope to be fully effective, particularly in an open society. Sadly, the putting of others before self is a feature that often seems to be lacking of both individuals and groups filling leadership roles – filling but not fulfilling in that their effectiveness is considerably degraded as a result.

| **Example is leadership.**

> *"Example is more efficacious than precept."*
> **Samuel Johnson**
>
> *"I must let them see that when I expose them I expose myself."*
> **Marlborough**
>
> *"Be an example to your men."*
> **Rommel**
>
> *"Example is leadership."*
> **Albert Schweitzer**

Selflessness and example come in many forms and can be displayed in many ways, both large and small. Instances of where these traits should have been shown but were not, perhaps inevitably gain more publicity than the reverse. Nevertheless there have been some instances in corporate life when boards and their members have acted in a self-centered way, regardless of what they were expecting from their workforce. In sport, there have been sad instances of individuals who are role models and therefore expected to lead by example, but who have failed in this crucial respect.

- We tend to hear more of selfishness and bad example than selflessness and good example.

- There has been a great deal of criticism of senior executives being awarded and accepting rewards far in excess of those given to their employees, yet they all contribute to the success of the organization. This is bad leadership.

- We seldom hear of the executives who refuse any increase – and there are a goodly number – when the corporate performance does not justify it, or of those companies where all share equally the fruits of success. But good news – or good leadership – is seldom newsworthy.

Good news – or good leadership – is seldom newsworthy.

Confidence

It is unlikely that any individual or group placed in a position of authority can exercise effective leadership if they are perceived to lack confidence either in themselves or their organization or whatever activity they are engaged in. This is not to suggest that effective leaders do not at times experience feelings of uncertainty and perhaps doubt – it would be unrealistic to expect otherwise. The important point is that this is not communicated to those whom they seek to lead; lack of confidence is contagious and quickly undermines effectiveness. Confidence does not have to be expressed in an extrovert way – a point often misunderstood by some who indulge in noisy expressions of authority. Under some circumstances quiet confidence and dignity is much more effective than any other style.

Confidence does not have to be expressed in an extrovert way.

"In confidence and quietness shall be your strength."

Isaiah

It is obvious that those who follow need themselves to have full confidence in the leader. In academic contexts it is confidence of an intellectual nature. In an applied leadership situation those who follow additionally need to feel fully confident that the leader has an understanding of their individual roles and that they themselves must have confidence in their leader's competence. This does not imply that the leader must be an expert in all the professional disciplines for which he or she might have overall responsibility: this would be an impossible task in most situations. What it does imply is that the leader must have an adequate understanding of those disciplines, their wider implications and how they impact on his or her leadership.

Intuition

The next attribute is probably the most difficult to describe. This is intuition, that sixth sense to know when things are not right or when to act. This ability is born of experience and judgment – and perhaps something indefinable.

"Intuition: *Immediate apprehension of the mind without reasoning; immediate apprehension by a sense; immediate insight.*"

Oxford English Dictionary

"*The quick recognition of a truth that the mind would ordinarily miss, or would perceive only after long study and reflection.*"

Von Clausewitz

Vision

Much has been written and said about vision or the "vision thing" in popular jargon. Since leadership is about giving direction, knowing where that direction is leading is all important. Yet many in senior leadership positions appear unable to articulate any sort of vision as to where their particular organization is going. Unfortunately the word "vision" itself has become part of the jargon, and has perhaps been overused and misused. Be that as it may, any group of people working together in any environment needs to have a clear idea of where their group is heading – and persuaded that it is in the right direction. We would not recommend what was once written about a young military officer on his periodic report by his superior "and his men follow him, if only out of curiosity."

> **Since leadership is about giving direction, knowing where that direction is leading is all important.**

"The very essence of leadership is ... to have a vision. It's got to be a vision you articulate clearly and forcefully on every occasion. You can't blow on an uncertain trumpet."
Quoted in *Thriving on Chaos* by Tom Peters

The use of the term "vision" at lower organizational levels is obviously inappropriate. Breadth of horizon seems more apt – that is the ability to think beyond the immediate environment and timeframe, and to put the work of the group into a wider context.

Ability to make decisions

An ability to make decisions is also among the fundamental requirements of an effective leader or leadership group. Some people appear fearful of the possible consequences of making a decision and do not want to be held accountable, should things not work out as hoped. They procrastinate. Yet not to have timely decisions leads rapidly to loss of group effectiveness and leader credibility. In practice decisions are seldom wholly right or wholly wrong. They often have to be made based as much on judgment as on a complete set of facts. The important thing is to have a decision.

The important thing is to have a decision.

> *"On the face of it the research division had everything going for it. Communication was good, people were consulted regularly, there was strong belief in the work being done. Yet, there was an underlying feeling of dissatisfaction amongst the managers. We discuss endlessly, but no-one will make a decision. It leads to endless frustration and delay."*
>
> **Pharmaceutical company (1993)**

Ability to simplify situations

An ability to simplify complex situations is another key attribute for leaders. When faced with complex situations, conflicting priorities and interests, large numbers of people and their emotions and a huge number of concurrent activities, it is easy to lose sense of purpose and direction. All things considered, leading usually requires in the event a single purpose and direction. To instill sufficient understanding and confidence among the persons involved, the leader frequently has to define and redefine the purpose and direction in the simplest of terms. This can of course be taken too far – many an inadequate leader oversimplifies the situation, forgets the purpose and loses direction. Clarity of thinking, particularly under pressure, is required. It is an ability that can and should be developed.

33

It is suggested that the above fundamental attributes constitute the invariable element of leadership; the need for them never changes. Furthermore they can be developed in people with the right coaching and training. A number are explored in greater depth in later chapters.

Performance check 1

THE LEADER

1 Are you able to identify clearly what is your management role, and your role as a leader?

2 What percentage of your time is spent in routine management, and what percentage fulfilling your leadership role? Should you increase the latter?

3 Are there any occasions when you feel that your team or organization have "cut moral corners," or you felt that you had to compromise your values? If so, have you confronted the issue?

4 Have you accepted *fully* responsibility for any decision made in your area of responsibility, or have you unfairly "passed the buck" on any occasion?

5 Do you feel that you are a good communicator? If not, are you taking any measures to improve your performance in this area?

6 Are you happy at your ability to make decisions, especially in complex situations, or do you tend to prevaricate over the process? If the latter, have you done anything to improve your decision-making skills?

Part II

THE LEADERSHIP FIELD

◆

Leadership: the action or influence necessary for the direction or organisation of effort in a group undertaking.

Oxford English Dictionary

◆

Chapter 4

◆

THE LEADERSHIP ENVIRONMENT

THE CHANGING ENVIRONMENT

While the attributes required by an effective leader may be constant, circumstances or the environment in which leadership is practiced may change or vary considerably, as may the factors influencing that environment.

Not to recognize the changing environment, or that the circumstances in which the leadership is being applied may differ from earlier experience, can lead rapidly to loss of leader effectiveness, or even leadership failure. It must be accepted that not all leaders are able to adjust to all circumstances – it would be unfair to expect it to be so – although the assumption is often made that they can. As a consequence, there have been numerous and often sad cases of leaders failing to live up to expectations: of successful military or business leaders failing in the political sphere: of leaders making an unsuccessful transition from public to private sector or vice versa; of leaders of large corporations being markedly less successful when moved to other large corporations in a different sector or perhaps to a smaller one. And even in the same organization, leaders who have been successful in one set of circumstances have had to be replaced when the environment has changed.

It is interesting to recall some of those "leaders" who were highly successful in running companies in the expansionist 1970s and 1980s. When consolidation was called for in the recession of the early 1990s, they could not sustain the momentum. They have disappeared. But these perhaps are the more extreme instances. Leadership is about direction which implies change. Leaders, to be effective, need themselves to be adaptable and accept change. And change occurs in many organizations on a daily basis.

Leaders, to be effective, need themselves to be adaptable and accept change.

Nevertheless, it must be acknowledged that all individuals have their limitations and that some are more suitable to one particular set of circumstances than another. That it should be desirable to change the leadership should not reflect unfairly on the individuals concerned. Not to change the leadership when such a move is patently necessary can have disastrous consequences for both organizations and individuals.

Following the Falklands War, the UK government decided to build a new airfield in the Falklands. The success of the project depended to a considerable extent on selecting and changing the project leaders for the different phases. The consortium responsible – Laing, Mowlem and Amey Roadstone – saw from the outset how a particular type of leader and style of leadership would be required during each phase. Three very different leaders were appointed – one for the pioneer phase, another for the project expansion period, and again a change when it turned into a major multisite operation. It was a model operation.

INFLUENCES ON THE LEADERSHIP ENVIRONMENT

Perhaps the most important influences on the leadership environment relate to social and sociological conditions. The period since the end of World War II has seen a dramatic improvement in education and an increased awareness amongst individuals of world and other events – based not least on a revolution in communication technology. This has led to increasing debate over issues, ranging from the highly significant to the most trivial, depending upon the point of view of individuals or groups. The desire for involvement in decision-making increases year by year with more and more people demanding accountability in ever increasing detail. The democratic process and detailed involvement has penetrated all aspects of life and work to an extent scarcely imagined even ten or twenty years ago, let alone a century. It has also led to a breaking down of social structures, changing attitudes to authority, and in some instances to a challenging of values. This has presented particular problems for some individuals, particularly those whose early experience was in very different circumstances. They feel that the acceptance of such social change is irreconcilable with their perception of leadership.

Good leaders however have always adapted to changed conditions and have relied on their effectiveness of personality rather than say, for example, unchallenged position, on the ability to persuade and influence rather than compel – in fact on the attributes outlined earlier. Regardless of the social changes, moreover, most people still accept that there are occasions when leadership has to be directive and an individual leader has to make decisions which are not based on

Good leaders have always adapted to changed conditions.

41

consensus, although they still need to be convinced of that decision if they are to respond wholeheartedly.

One of the most enduring misconceptions of leadership in many spheres is that it has to be an authoritarian and insensitive concept. The situation is not helped by a small minority who interpret it that way. Obviously some leadership has strong legal backing (for example, military commanders have considerable legal powers of sanction), and other leaders have powers of economic sanction (for example, employers who hire and fire freely). In reality effective leaders in all spheres seldom take recourse to a book of rules or resort to sanction.

Culture

A further influence that can have a marked effect on leadership practice is culture – national, regional, organizational, professional or gender. Anyone who has worked in an international environment, for example, is aware of the cultural differences that exist between nations, even though they may share a common interest. Not to make due allowance for those differences usually results in less than effective leadership. It is a problem faced by international commercial organizations, and to a lesser extent, by multidisciplinary project teams. We cover this in Chapters 7 and 10.

Technology

Improvements in technology particularly in the field of communications, have an impact that both helps and potentially impedes. On the one hand, technology can affect information flow and decision-making and greatly facilitate control. On the other hand it increases the ability to interfere and to demand an instant reporting of events, developments few at any level can afford to ignore.

Some changes brought about by technology that can affect leadership

- An increasing number of jobs can be physically decentralized (including to the home) for example that of telephone operator or software designer.

- Some of the extended supporting team can be the other side of the world; for example, UK-based travel agencies being supported by accounts staff in India.

- There can be instant communication from the remote site to the corporate headquarters and vice versa.

- The politician or senior executive can be the other side of the world in a matter of hours, should a difficult situation arise which they could influence.

- Television portrays the news immediately from the point of crisis to the general public, leading often to demands for instant leadership decisions, bypassing any hierarchical structure.

Technology also enables organizational structures to be changed. In industry and commerce this has led to flatter structures and decentralization of decision-making and many of the other leadership functions. It is almost certain that institutions will follow suit – despite a desire to keep traditional hierarchical structures, not least because of the demands for "answerability." Re-engineering, after all, is redesigning and adapting structures for better leadership practice throughout the organization.

Organizational role

Organizations and organizational structures are obviously influenced too by role, as is the type of leadership required. There is a marked difference in the style of leadership required in a research organization in comparison with a manufacturing company. The state of the organization is also a factor: whether it is expanding or declining, new, mature or in a poor state. It is fairly generally accepted that not all leaders can adapt readily to all organizational environments – it would be unreasonable to expect that to be the case.

Organizational task

Leadership is also affected by the task faced by a group, by the composition of the group itself and by the personality and gender of the group leader. Crisis management demands a different leadership style and the use of different techniques to those required in routine tasks. Military people, quite rightly, tend to be selected for their ability to lead in crises or adverse circumstances. However, many of the situations others face in leadership terms are of a noncrisis and nonoperational nature – but they often tackle them as if they were. Failure to adapt to such changes in circumstances must indicate a lack of leadership capacity and perhaps raise questions about the selection process. This is not to gainsay the need to identify leaders who are particularly good in crisis situations and place them where their aptitude can best be used.

Personality

Any organization or team is comprised of a number of (often markedly) different personalities. The individual team members and team leaders are changed from time to time, and the individuals themselves change in their reaction to different situations. Thus the collective personality of each team is different and everchanging. To be effective a leader must be able to recognize and react to these differences and changes and to the different needs of the individual components.

LEADERSHIP LEVEL

The type and style of leadership required is also affected by the level at which it is being applied or practiced.

Leaders at the lower levels usually have a much more direct relationship (physically and organizationally) with those they lead. It is they who tackle the day-to-day and hour-to-hour problems and their preoccupation is more with the short-term than the long. Leaders at this level are often inexperienced, or until recently were perhaps one of the led.

Leaders further up the spectrum may be one or two layers removed from direct control and usually have to adjust to working through others, which in itself some find difficult. They may have responsibility for more than one team, possibly involving different disciplines, with competing and sometimes conflicting demands. The leader's problems are often compounded by physical and geographical separation. They are still concerned with day-to-day affairs, but have to consider more the longer term.

Arguably, in leadership terms, the middle of the spectrum is the most critical level. In industry certainly it is recognized as the area giving most cause for concern. Do the people there have a real job? Are there intangible benefits brought by middle managers which will be missed if they are pushed out? There is a tendency for those at this level to be resistant to change (although they are usually those most responsible for implementing it), to feel most pressured, and for them to become administrators rather than leaders.

> **Arguably, in leadership terms, the middle of the spectrum is the most critical level.**

45

The disappearing/reappearing middle manager

To some writers the problem of middle management is a non-issue: they have abolished it as part of their re-engineering, delayering, slimming down process. Middle management does, however, have a vital role to play – and is being reinvented by some of those who previously advocated its demise. Senior executives and junior managers have not been able to take over the whole function. This is not to suggest that there is not ample scope for reducing some layers of middle management, but ridding an organization of good people for no better purpose than reducing numbers just for the sake of it, is foolish.

"There is a real drive to eliminate management posts within BT. ... They've been pushing out managers over 50. You lose a lot of experience that way."

Professor Jim Dorcan, Ashridge Management College

"Companies may come to rue the day they swept away their middle managers so ruthlessly. In many cases they've cut out managers who made important contributions in areas such as training."

Professor Bernard Taylor, Henley Management College
from *The Times*, April 8, 1993

"In many companies we hear ... 'Top management is the barrier to change.' There is much that middle management can do to take the initiative. If they wait for top management ... they are themselves engaging in behaviour that is exactly the opposite of what is required. ... Change can start anywhere in the organisation and spread, as results become evident to others."

Alan L. Frohman and Leonard W. Johnson (1993)[7]

If some or all middle managers positively assist in spreading good leadership practice throughout the company, then their individual and collective leadership function must be recognized and encouraged. Leadership at the top also has an added dimension in both a political and civic representational sense.

At the more senior levels leaders have to take a wider view and their preoccupation is with the longer term, although there is still a need to monitor the present and sometimes focus on the shorter term. They are more often faced with conflicts in priorities and are answerable for performance – to repeat President Truman's words "it's where the buck stops."

> **Those at the top of the organizations are the ones who should create the vision, establish the objectives, and set the standards by which the organization is to operate.**

Those at the top of the organizations are the ones who should create the vision, establish the objectives, and set the standards by which the organization is to operate. They are generally removed from day-to-day concerns, yet may still be answerable for current activity or performance. They have a need to communicate regularly with all members of their organization without undermining the intermediate structure, but are often inhibited from doing so by formalities that can become barriers.

DIMENSIONS OF LEADERSHIP

Leadership is sometimes regarded as only having a single aspect, yet analysis suggests that it has at least two. One aspect is concerned with creating a vision or identifying the long-term goals for an organization, and with the developing of a strategy for the fulfillment of that vision or the attainment of those goals.

47

Leadership is also concerned with making important decisions related to that vision and those goals. The other aspect is concerned more with the shorter term, with group dynamics and with working within the strategy.

To be successful, organizations need leadership of both kinds. Individual leaders often have greater strength in one aspect and are perhaps less effective in the other. For them to be effective in the round, such people need to be complemented by others in their teams who compensate for their areas of relative weakness. In commercial life this often leads to the sharing of leadership at the top, with a chairman concerned with the strategic and external dimensions, and a chief executive focusing on the day to day and shorter term. This aspect is explored further in Chapter 12.

Chapter 5

◆

THE LED

UNDERSTANDING PEOPLE

For some years now we have witnessed the steady growth of human resource management as a specialized area of management. While this may have improved the focus on people generally, the act of institutionalizing the handling of people has obscured and confused many of the real aspects of human motivation, including the fact that people continue to need to be led as well as managed.

> **People continue to need to be led as well as managed.**

It has been stressed already that all organizations are much more reliant on the willpower of their people – at all levels – than is generally realized. Normally the chief concerns are capital, financial ratios, corporate plans, and human resource management in the abstract. Most small, medium and even large companies are highly personality intensive,[8] in that people's emotions, energies and potential to work at a high level of performance rely on the way they interact. We are talking here about real, living people.

> **We are talking here about real, living people.**

All of us experience and display at different times strong desires and frustrations, heights of imagination and depths of despair, cynicism or indifference, superhuman energy or virtual paralysis.

One of the bases of effective leadership is an understanding of people. This may be regarded as a restatement of the obvious, but it is not an infrequent experience to meet people in positions of leadership who do not understand or accept this fundamental tenet. They seldom perform effectively as leaders.

People need to be emotionally stimulated to perform effectively any activity. Some of that stimulation or motivation is self-generated, the extent depending on the individual and the circumstances. In the group or team situation motivation needs to be enhanced (or in some cases actually induced) externally by the organization or leader, especially if any perceived risk, threat or challenge is involved or there is a need to sublimate personal interest and inclination to that of the group.

Regardless of cultural and other influences, and of the fact that all human beings are different from one another in terms of personality, fundamentally we all have similar physiological and psychological needs, and that we are often motivated or discouraged by similar factors or circumstances. Sadly, the focus of many organizations and companies seems to be primarily on appealing to or satisfying physiological and material needs. This disregards the fact that the most powerful motivators tend to be psychological, most of which can be provided by good leadership.

The most powerful motivators tend to be psychological, most of which can be provided by good leadership.

"People are motivated primarily by money. We pay managers well and expect them to perform well – and we shoot the stragglers."

This statement (1989) was made by the managing director of a large group of multiproduct companies. It was amongst the first to go into receivership, when the recession hit its markets.

This also seems to be the view in many large commercial companies too with regard particularly to executive reward and an acceptance of individual greed as a prime motivator. Arguably, the acceptance of material rewards that are perceived by others to be unjustified has done a great deal to undermine leader credibility in some companies and pays scant regard to the general level of sophistication of people.

Getting the best out of people

We believe that above a certain level of material reward, the job itself – its challenges and potential for achievement – is by far the most powerful spur to a majority of people. This is not unworldly idealism, but is borne out by extensive research and real experience. It does not mean of course that people do not expect to be fairly rewarded: but this is only part of what they want.

The widely quoted American clinical psychologist, Frederick Herzberg,[9] listed the five prime motivators of people as being:

- achievement;
- recognition;
- attraction of the work itself;
- responsibility;
- advancement or personal growth;

51

and the main causes of dissatisfaction as being:

- company policy;
- administration;
- supervision and nonrecognition;
- salary;
- interpersonal relationships;
- working conditions.

He noted that the removal of the cause of dissatisfaction does not necessarily act as a motivator.

Motivation

"Suddenly I realised that I was spending the bulk of my time 'managing' other people's aspirations – customers, staff, shareholders. You have to drive out the fear that they won't achieve what they want. Often I have to help people articulate what their real aspirations are."

Philip Horton, Chairman, Dewramet

"We encourage our staff to work at a high energy level, and they respond. Really only those who want to work here, do. In this business where there are narrow profit margins we have to work hard and this is achieved by good team-work. We spend a lot of money on training. There has to be a bit of 'fear' around or you will really not get the best out of people. Our centre managers have to be leaders: they cannot just be good organisers.

Setting a personal example is the key to being a good leader, and it takes hard work to maintain the best example at all times."

Tom Farmer, Chairman, KWIK-FIT plc

From the point of view of effective leadership it is important to recognize the symptoms of unfulfilled needs and the absence of sufficient motivators:

- high rates of absenteeism and sick leave;
- poor timekeeping;
- resistance to change;
- clockwatching;
- unmet deadlines or production targets;
- demarcation disputes;
- withdrawal of labour;
- poor quality work.

> **Setting a personal example is the key to being a good leader, and it takes hard work to maintain the best example at all times.**

In nearly all cases these can be attributed to indifferent or poor leadership.

> *"An astonishing £800 million of taxpayers' money would be saved if public sector sick leave were brought down to private sector levels."*
>
> **CBI Survey (1995)**

> *"The best indicators I have of unit leadership and morale are to be found in the hospital and police reports."*
>
> **An Army General**

One of the problems in industry has been the absence of a real leadership structure: of leaders and teams with whom people can identify. This is now being recognized, and it is interesting how the Rover Group, for example, has restructured around small teams each with its own leader – an enormous change from previous practice in an industry which was based on very large production lines and which placed the emphasis on coercion and regulation rather than leadership.

RECOGNIZING PEOPLE'S CONTRIBUTION

Considering how little effort (and cost) is involved, and the potential effect, it is surprising how often individual and group contribution and achievement go unrecognized. It costs nothing to say "thank you," or "well done;" all it requires is a little thought. The impact it can make, on the other hand, can be considerable.

> **It costs nothing to say 'thank you,' or 'well done;' all it requires is a little thought.**

The Unipart Group of Companies (UGC), a world class company in its field and acknowledged as one that puts a high value on its workforce, places considerable emphasis on formal recognition of contribution and achievement. Presentations at which all directors are present are made on a regular basis. Importantly, that recognition is not based on material reward.

Knowing people

While we may all share common needs, we are still different from one another, some of us markedly so. We all have different personalities, interests, priorities, and to some degree motivations. And we all have different pressures on us. Moreover, our lives are generally compartmentalized, and we are sometimes different people (not least because we fill different roles) at work, at home and at play. Yet, we frequently make judgments on people based only on one part of their lives, perhaps their working persona,

> **We all have different pressures on us.**

which may involve perhaps no more than 25 per cent of their time.

To try to get to know people better as individuals is not being intrusive, although some might use that as a reason for not doing so. It is one of the recognized actions of a good leader.

Simple test used in our consultancy work

Interviewees are asked:

- What does A do in his or her spare time?

- What are B's family circumstances?

- At what stage are C's children at?

- When is your secretary's birthday?

The embarrassed lack of knowledge shown by some was quite revealing and in many cases matched up with poor team performance.

People's reactions

People also react differently to individual leaders and leadership styles. It is important, therefore that those seeking to be effective leaders are sensitive to their effect on others – and to their acceptability as leader, something that should not be assumed – without becoming over self-conscious. This requires a means of gauging such feelings and a seeking of feedback that is accurate and not sycophantic. Those of more mature years might find this approach difficult to accept – the "I am as I am" school. This is being made culturally easier and will ultimately become more acceptable, particularly in those organizations in which there is a trend towards peer group and upwards assessment.

In reality no leader will go far wrong if he or she obeys two simple rules:

1 Don't patronize. No one enjoys being implicity made to feel inferior.

2 Value people for their contribution and value them equally. The secret is to make people feel more valued without being more valuable than any other team member.

PROBLEM PEOPLE

No team is ever perfect, and every leader is faced at some time with an individual team member who might be categorized as a "problem"– although the rest of the team appears to be working well. This can occur at any level.

The first inclination of many is to choose to ignore the issue in the hope that it will go away, which it seldom does. Such a reaction is perfectly understandable since the prospect of a possible confrontation causes most people a degree of stress. But continuing to ignore the issue can lead to much greater problems: the leader risks undermining not only his or her authority, but also in the longer term the cohesion and effectiveness of the whole team.

At the other extreme is the resort to sanction. Such a measure should be used sparingly, and as a last rather than a first resort. Sadly, it is often the latter. A leader who feels he constantly has to exert his authority and compel subordinates is diminishing the power of their self-discipline and willing compliance. As suggested

The use of heavy-handed sanction and punishment is the antithesis of good leadership.

earlier, the use of heavy-handed sanction and punishment is the antithesis of good leadership.

Where it is in their power to do so, some people choose to get rid of the problem by having the person moved – often to become another team's problem. Obviously, in some cases such a course may be essential or ultimately become necessary. In other instances it may not be an option, and in any case no such action should ever be taken until the problem has been addressed with the individual concerned, uncomfortable though that might be. It requires a degree of moral courage and is something most would rather avoid and, sadly often do, even the outwardly most confident.

Surprisingly perhaps, some appear unaware that they have become a problem or have failed to appreciate the possible consequences both to themselves and others. Finding the cause may not be easy. It is important to choose the time and place carefully – public confrontations are not to be recommended – and to be prepared to listen carefully and to explain. There may, for instance, be a communication problem, and a need to clarify roles and positions. The leader must be prepared for possible personal criticism. Indeed, the leader may unwittingly be the problem or at least part of it.

The leader must be prepared for possible personal criticism.

There may be an interpersonal conflict or an insensitivity to personal feelings. The leader may be perceived as a bully or as one who undervalues others – and is often both surprised and hurt to be told so.

Differing perceptions

People are often amazed that what seems to them a small or insignificant matter can assume major proportions to others, and have a totally disproportionate effect on interpersonal relationships. Sometimes the realization can be very late in the day. The problem often concerns status, reward or lack of recognition of effort, and can involve an imagined slight, which may have been unthinking rather than deliberate. The problem is usually made worse by an unwillingness on the part of the injured party to mention the matter. It festers on, generating increasing resentment and ill feeling.

Leaders must be sensitive, good observers and active listeners, to avoid unintentional injury. However, the leader must not surrender his or her authority.

PEOPLE WITH PROBLEMS

The problem person may of course be a person with a problem. Most people are faced with personal problems of one sort or another – domestic, financial, health, etc. Most endeavor to keep them away from their work and indeed often throw themselves into work to forget their problems. The last thing they want is to reminded of them.

Getting it wrong

"I was shattered by my normally equable secretary's reaction when I tentatively enquired about a family problem I knew she was faced with. It was like a slap in the face. I really should have known better than ask. If only I had thought."

Managing Director (1989)

The good leader should nevertheless be aware of the problems faced by any member of the team and even when not wishing to interfere in any way will make due allowances – without unfairly overburdening the rest of the team.

Some, of course, seek advice which displays a confidence in the leader. It can also be taken as a form of flattery by the leader. It is an area in which, if not careful, one can quickly get out of one's depth, and allocate a disproportionate amount of one's time and effort.

There are others who do wish to burden the rest of the team with their problems, or whose work becomes seriously affected. In which case, the person with the problem becomes a problem person, and should be dealt with accordingly.

The last resort

"I had been in charge of the organization for a short period but already had time to appreciate that one of the divisions was performing badly. I went through the process of twice warning the head of the division, who was also a director, that I had to have an improvement – which he promised but did not deliver. A few weeks later it was reported to me that he was the worse for drink when he should have been working and that he was making a fool of himself in front of his subordinates. I sent for him, discovered that he was unfit for work, relieved him of his position but also arranged for him to see a doctor. I did not enjoy the next few hours as I was sensitive to the consequences of what I had done – it would mean the end of his career with the organization. It was almost a relief some hours later to learn that he had been admitted to a clinic as someone with a major alcohol problem. I probably saved his life. What really irritated me was that I then discovered that his problem was well known and had been hidden by well-meaning colleagues. He had been quietly moved around, and no one had bothered to do anything about it."

Chief Executive's experience

Performance check 2

THE LED RESPOND

1 Are people in your organization given sufficient recognition as individuals?

2 Are people's achievements and performance adequately acknowledged?

3 Is the organization's culture based on trust or mistrust of the individual?

4 Is sufficient emphasis placed on providing good working conditions?

5 Are people frustrated by seemingly needless bureaucracy?

6 Are you faced with labor or demarcation disputes? If so, have you determined the **real** causes?

7 Do you have concerns about the quality of output?

Chapter 6

◆

TEAMS

LEADERSHIP AND TEAMS

*"**Leadership**. The action or influence necessary for the direction or organisation of effort to a group undertaking."*
Oxford English Dictionary

Leadership in its true sense does not exist in isolation. It is dependent on the interaction of two or more people. That interaction may be direct and immediate – as in the case of a sports team – or more remote, for example in moral or intellectual leadership. Too often, however, the linkage is ignored or underemphasized. It is an error made frequently, for instance, by those purporting to assess leadership potential in others.

Successful leadership can usually be assessed in terms of its effects on others either as individual followers, or, in the sense that we are considering it, in terms of group or team performance. In the latter case a successful team can be said to have an effectiveness or output that is greater than the sum effectiveness of its component parts. All too often however the opposite is encountered: a team whose effectiveness is perceived to be less,

> **A successful team can be said to have an effectiveness or output that is greater than the sum effectiveness of its component parts.**

sometimes far less, than that of the potential output of its individual members added together. It is easy and common enough in the circumstances to blame poor team performance on individual team members or the team's chemistry. The truth is, it is a failure of leadership.

A team may start off as a group. While the two may have some features in common, the distinguishing characteristics of the team are that it exists to fulfill a common task which its individual members cannot achieve on their own, and that it has an identified leader (or leaders). This typifies the boardroom team, the assembly line team, the project team – or the sports club team.

A team

"Group, with common purpose, complementary skills, interdependence" (Dictionary definition).

"A collection of differences" (Professor Charles Handy).

The authors of the book *The Wisdom of Teams* differentiate strongly between groups and teams. They emphasize that a real team, one that performs effectively, must be developed from a group of individuals, and that the group has posi-tively incorporated itself into a team with the "disciplined application of 'team basics.'"[10] (John R. Katzenbach and Douglas K. Smith

---

Types and sizes of teams

Teams are formed for a variety of purposes. In a typical company, for example, one may find management teams, production teams, specialist teams, etc. Some have a more or less permanent existence while others, such as project teams, may have a limited life span – once their objective has been achieved or removed their *raison d'être*, their binding force, disappears and the group usually ceases to be a team.

Group dynamics

Group dynamics, the serious study of how a collection of people behave when working together for some end or meeting for some social purpose, came to maturity in the 1950s.[11] As a subject it includes group membership, pressures for unity and conformity, power and influence, motivational processes, formal and informal structures and "pecking orders." These have been deeply researched, though they have not always been connected to the study and practice of leadership.

To be effective and manageable, teams should be kept reasonably small – usually not more than eight or ten. Larger than that they can become unwieldy and break up into smaller groups, introducing unnecessary divisiveness or damaging dissention. Too large a team may discourage active participation, leading to feelings of frustration or wasted time. Chairmen and managers in these increasingly competitive times are now beginning to appreciate the wisdom of looking closely at team size and composition.

Extended teams

There is a strong tendency in most of us to identify only with our immediate team, be it the board or work group. Most organizations consist of a multiplicity of teams, many interdependent and all part of the corporate team. And it is worth considering that the corporate team, like a chain, may only be as strong as its weakest link. The secretary, the receptionist, the cleaner are as much part of the corporate team as the executive or direct wealth creator and need to be treated as such. But how often do we find, for example, that our initial contact is unwelcoming or ill–informed (or both) – clear indication of lack of team identity and poor leadership.

> **The secretary, the receptionist, the cleaner are as much part of the corporate team as the executive or direct wealth creator and need to be treated as such.**

What is the team?

The consultant was tasked with improving the effectiveness of a hospital's working. He found that the surgical, ward and administrative teams worked in complete isolation, causing particularly waste of valuable theater time. No one had ever bothered to look at it as a total activity, and the suggestion that this should take place was bitterly resented. As to the mere fact of going away together to look at means of improving ...

At no stage of training or subsequently had any effort been made to explain the role and needs of any of the other teams.

Team culture

In the past considerable emphasis was placed on the importance of teams and teamplaying. It was certainly part of the ethos of

UK schools (and still is in some), although in the state sector over the past four decades such an attitude had been rejected by many, as running counter to the prevailing philosophy of education. And in recent years team culture has not featured strongly within industrial and commercial culture. Indeed the opposite has often been the case: in many organizations we have seen the growth of a positive anti–team culture and of a cult of individualism, in which individuals' personal aspirations (or "private agendas" in the current jargon) have seemed to predominate. In these circumstances information, which should be shared for the common good is often used as a basis for a form of power broking.

Things are changing in the better companies and organizations, and the word "team" has now reentered the corporate vocabulary from boardroom down to production unit. There is a growing realization – a rediscovery – that working in close harmony is much more effective (and more profitable in every sense) than coming together in a somewhat ad hoc fashion. At bottom, too, most individuals themselves want to identify with and be a member of a team –it is part of human nature. Some of course do not; they have an antipathy toward any form of group involvement. While the latter may have their place in the general order of things, it certainly should not be in any corporate activity. But such people are in a very small minority.

There is a growing realization – a rediscovery – that working in close harmony is much more effective (and more profitable in every sense).

THE NATURE OF TEAMS

In some ways teams are similar to individuals. Like individuals, teams have personalities, develop work habits, and acquire neuroses. But they react more slowly to stimuli than do individuals, their responses tend to be more predictable, and they appear to be more vulnerable to change especially to a change of leadership.

Teams are seldom in a fixed or static state; most are in a state of almost continuous change or development. That change is sometimes slow and almost imperceptible, sometimes dramatic.

> **Like individuals, teams have personalities, develop work habits, and acquire neuroses.**

Some of the change is evolutionary as a team matures. Any group or team is likely to go through four stages of development which can affect considerably how it performs and behaves. These stages can be roughly summarized as:

- Stage one, the foundation stage, when the team is still a collection of individuals rather than a cohesive unit. The focus is on determining purpose, group composition, personality, life span and modus operandi, with each individual member wishing to establish his or her own identity, role and contribution.

- Stage two, the initial operating or settling-down phase when the original arrangements may prove unworkable or are challenged. Difficulties may arise as personal agendas come to the surface, or as leadership and other roles, operating procedures, and even purpose are questioned, and interpersonal hostility may be generated. If successfully handled this second stage ends with a new and more realistic set of objectives, procedures and norms.

- Stage three is a maturing or developing phase, as the team's collective personality evolves together with improvements in communications, procedures, decision–making. Ideally, group commitment increases and overall effectiveness grows. As in any maturing process there are still challenges and occasional difficulties.

- Stage four is that of full maturity when the team realizes its potential. However, teams are unlikely to remain permanently at the fourth stage once having achieved it. Some reversion to an earlier stage(s) is almost inevitable as circumstances or individuals change. Equally likely, other teams may never get beyond stages two or three.

Professor Charles Handy, in his book *Understanding Organisations*, summarizes the stages pithily as "forming, storming, norming, and performing."

The important point for leaders to appreciate is that this evolutionary or development process takes place, and the general char-

"Forming, storming, norming, and performing."

acteristics of each phase. Certainly it is quite easy to relate our own experience of teams to those stages of development, especially where the team's life, purpose and composition were fixed. One can recall, for instance, how individuals grew in their roles, as they and the team matured and the work they did developed successfully.

Change can also be caused by a re–establishment of goals, new operating conditions, and perhaps most frequently by the comings and goings in team membership; even one person being replaced can lead to a dramatic change in a team's chemistry and

Change is usually good for teams.

collective personality. Small, closely knit specialist teams are particularly vulnerable in the latter case and often suffer a dramatic drop in effectiveness when one of their number leaves.

Change is usually good for teams. Indeed it is sometimes deemed necessary to introduce change into teams that have become too inward–looking, out of balance, or even too interdependent.

TEAM COMPOSITION

In the definitions quoted earlier appear the key words and phrases "complementary skills," "interdependence" and "collection of differences." Yet experience suggests that these fundamental aspects are often ignored or disregarded. As a consequence, many teams seem unbalanced, and appear less than fully effective. They lack what is called synergy, a property of effective teams, discussed below.

Realistically speaking some leaders may not be able to influence directly the composition of their own teams: they are predetermined, usually by appointment, and especially at the lower levels of an hierarchical structure. But even in the latter circumstances they can be balanced, in personality terms at least, by those at a higher level responsible for individual appointments. This perhaps begs the question: is it best anyway for leaders to select their own teams, or would it be better to have their teams selected for them by a person or group of people who are able to take a more objective view? Arguably the latter course is desirable and at any level. The record of those selecting their own teams is not good. This is a theme we shall return to later.

But what is the ideal team? What should it consist of? As suggested in the quotes, it is a complementary balance of both contribution and personality relevant to the task. In Dr Meredith Belbin's book *Management Teams: Why They Succeed or Fail*, which is based on extensive research, he suggests that effective teams appear to be made up of people who are able to fulfil nine identifiable roles. These are:

1 **The Coordinator [or Chairman].** A person with a strong sense of objectives, a good communicator and judge of people. One who is calm and self-controlled.

2 **The Shaper.** Someone with drive and a readiness to challenge. Likely to be outgoing, dynamic and perhaps highly strung, and somewhat impatient.

3 **The Plant.** A person with good intellect, imagination and knowledge. May be a little impractical and inclined to be introverted.

4 **The Monitor–Evaluator.** The hardheaded unemotional analytical type.

5 **The Resource Investigator.** An extrovert enthusiastic person, people orientated, perhaps more easily bored than most.

6 **The Implementer.** A practical and hardworking person with lots of common sense and good organizational ability.

7 **The Team Worker.** A likeable person who is good at getting people to work together. Not one to take the lead or be decisive in a crisis.

8 **The Completer-finisher.** Conscientious, painstaking, something of a worrier, tends to become overconcerned with minutiae.

9 **The Expert** or **Specialist.** Someone who has been enlisted for particular skills, expertise or knowledge.

In truth a person will have more than one and often a number of these skills in different proportions, as part of their personality and inclinations. An effective team does not need nine members, indeed studies of group dynamics recommend a task team (as opposed to a discussion group) achieves most with between five and seven members.

Professor Charles Handy reduces the list of types to four:

1 **A Captain.**

2 **A Driver.**

3 **An Administrator.**

4 **A Worker.**

Others suggest captain, innovator, pragmatist, conciliator, and subject expert. The point to emphasize is that teams need to have a balance of personalities, skills and experience if they are to be fully effective. Teams of clones and sycophants – and even star performers – seldom are. Yet there is a marked tendency, particularly in specialist organizations and in top level teams, to avoid balance – or as some might see it, to avoid conflict or tension – and to include those who are similar in outlook and personality, or who perhaps will not rock the boat.

A useful exercise for the reader might be to evaluate the team(s) of which he/she is a member against Belbin and Handy's models and in terms of effectiveness.

Thatcher's teams

To the outside observer, Margaret Thatcher's earlier Cabinets, which contained a wide range and balance of personality types (as well as representing a number of different political interests), were far more effective as teams than those in her later administrations, which appeared to consist of people of relatively similar dispositions. Using Belbin's types, the later Cabinets lacked arguably a second shaper to challenge her, a coordinator, a good team worker, and perhaps a plant.

SELECTING TEAM MEMBERS

It is relatively rare for a leader to be in a position to select his or her own team completely freely and from scratch. Even when faced with setting up a new project team, there are usually constraints as to who might be available. More likely, it is a question of changing the composition and balance of an existing team as and when an opportunity occurs such as a team member leaving. Obviously, there are occasions when more proactive measures need to be taken – for instance when a team is consistently or unacceptably underperforming. New team leaders are sometimes appointed for this purpose.

In those instances where there is no choice, certainly in the short term, it is the job of the leader to remedy the shortfall or imbalance by trying to develop the team both individually and collectively, if necessary with external assistance, minimizing the weaknesses and building on its strengths.

When the opportunity does arise to appoint a new member(s) it is nearly always worth seeking the views of people outside the group for their opinion of the team, and especially in terms of personality balance. The dangers of the leader doing the task without advice are several:

- it is difficult for the leader to be fully objective, especially if the leader has been with the team for some time;

- few leaders know themselves sufficiently well to be able to select balancing personalities;

- it is human nature to select people whom we like, or think we will get on well with. Mostly, we do not welcome potential conflict or contrariness;

- there is a marked tendency to select people whom we think will "fit in" – which can mean many things.

Team membership

A possible danger of focussing on team leadership is that we forget that team leaders are also team members of both their own and other teams. There they may not be the leader. Too often in fact leaders do not see themselves as team members, with a conse-

Team leaders are also team members of both their own and other teams.

quent reduction in their own effectiveness. In the commercial world particularly executives can normally expect to be members of several teams, each with its own purpose, personality, chemistry and lifespan – and each potentially demanding a different contribution. A number of chairmen and chief executives have remarked on a particular problem they have encountered: that of reconciling a perceived conflict of interest some executives experience (albeit unconsciously) between membership of teams at different levels. They instance the divisional director who is the leader of his own team (with its parochial interests) and a member of the board with its much wider interest.

Team membership

An interesting historical example of an outstanding leader whose fullest potential was curtailed by an inability to operate effectively as a member of someone else's team was General Montgomery. He was brilliant in North Africa where he could concentrate on his own team and his own campaign. In North West Europe, where as well as running his own team he was also a member of Eisenhower's, with its wider remit and the conflicting priorities of its component members, he was far less successful.

Good and not so good teams

Most people have experienced being a member of both successful and unsuccessful teams, and it is worth reflecting on why the teams performed as they did. Although not immediately obvious, most would agree in the end that leadership was a major factor, if not the most important. This is as true at national level as it is in organizations or companies.

Effective teams

A test of effective team leadership is to make a group of people into a team, and then collectively to produce results which could not be produced by individuals. Often the results or objectives are beyond individual achievement or impossible, other than through teamwork. The dynamics of teamwork can be ascribed to the synergy of people working together.

A test of effective team leadership is to make a group of people into a team, and then collectively to produce results which could not be produced by individuals.

Synergy

Some people have difficulty with the term "synergy." It is usually defined as the team's (or company's) combined and interrelated efforts being greater than the sum of individual efforts. With regard to collective leadership, we do not believe this goes far enough to describe a very powerful internal team dynamic. True synergy is the interrelating and multiplying effect of individual effort. The effect is incremental and in many contexts measurable.

True synergy is the interrelating and multiplying effect of individual effort.

Negative synergy is when the potential for incremental effect is diminished or destroyed, because the interrelation of effort fails to work. Usually this is because the individuals are not good team members, and their aspirations or priorities conflict. As often as not the team disintegrates.

Perhaps the most noticeable thing about effective and successful teams is the atmosphere in which they operate and which they generate. They have an absence of divisive tensions and artificial barriers. There is an acceptance of and commitment to

73

the task and no sign of disinterest, dissatisfaction or boredom. The team is confident yet relaxed, full of self-respect, ambitious, healthily competitive, and has high expectations. Relationships are good both between the leader and the team, among the team members, and with other teams.

Within the team there is mutual support and trust of members, which usually extends beyond the team's operating environment. At the same time there is respect for differences in individual contributions, values and personalities. This leads to openness and frankness in discussion and acceptance of decisions (even though they may not accord with individuals' opinions), in the knowledge that all points of view have been listened to. Importantly, the team is happy regularly and honestly to review performance in seeking to improve its effectiveness.

An effective team

"It was the happiest and most satisfying period of my professional life. Because of the way in which the chief executive (our team leader) operated we really got our act together and as a result had the satisfaction of achieving a great deal. We really were as one. There was complete openness and trust, very little carping, never any recrimination, and a spirit of 'we're all in it together.' We worked really hard, and long hours, but no–one seemed to mind. Our team spirit extended well beyond the work place and we all became good friends and did a lot together socially, even sharing holidays. We meet as a group still."

One happy experience. Have you never been as fortunate – and wondered why?

Less effective teams

In those teams that are less effective the atmosphere is seldom relaxed or friendly. Individual team members often appear to focus on themselves and their own goals rather than those of the team. At root it is a matter of lack of openness, and poor interpersonal relationships. Goals are unclear or unaccepted; there often appears to be a gulf or little rapport between teamleader and team. Roles and relationships are unclear; team members appear suspicious of one another's motives. There are undercurrents of hostility and antagonism and splinter groups often form. Individuals appear frustrated and consequently dissatisfied with their work. Unhelpful competition exists between individual team members and with other teams. Meetings are unproductive and not welcomed. The impression is given that the leader does not listen and is uncomfortable with discussion, which he or she sees as a challenge to their authority.

The net outcome is disjointed effort, unmet targets, a lack of creativity and initiative, and low morale. There is no group cohesion, little social intercourse outside the workplace, and little concern for the individual.

An ineffective team

"It's not an experience I want to go through too often. Looking back on it, we really were a bit of a disaster as a team. Somehow or other we never really got our act together. Most of the time we didn't really know what was expected of us or who was calling the shots – we were often given different and conflicting orders by different people. Dissatisfaction started coming through in all sorts of ways – although this may have not seemed the case at the time. Several asked to go to other jobs, using a variety of

75

what were pretty thin reasons. There was a lot of backbiting against Chris the team leader and against other individuals. I had more time off sick than at any time in my career. Our work seemed more a matter of crisis (and often disaster) management than an orderly process. Chris was a nice enough guy – in fact probably too nice – but he did not seem to be in charge or even want to be."

This was a less happy experience, and sadly one that is too frequent.

TENSION AND CONFLICT IN TEAMS

It is very unlikely that any team will consist entirely of like minded people. Indeed as has already been suggested such a situation would probably be undesirable from the point of view of team effectiveness. People are very different from one another and while they might agree on a common aim and a common course of action for the team, their individual priorities, motivation, values and cultural backgrounds might vary considerably. This could (indeed is likely to) give rise at times to an element of tension within the group, a factor any leader must be sensitive to. Too often, however, leaders make the assumption that all members of their team are similar to themselves in both outlook and priorities.

In an open and effective team that tension can be creative. It is accepted and welcomed. Yet in practice some feel threatened by its presence. The leader's job is to manage and capitalize on the tension – and not to try to pretend it does not exist, or endeavor to suppress it. Not to have an element of tension might suggest complacency, an overdominant leader or a team of sycophants.

On occasion, tension goes beyond the creative stage and starts to exert a negative influence. It can lead to damaging conflict if not controlled by the leader, especially when an individual or individuals challenge the direction a team is taking or the way in which it is going about its task, refuse to accede to the corporate

> **On occasion, tension goes beyond the creative stage and starts to exert a negative influence.**

needs of the team or are in fundamental disagreement with other members of the team. Such has been the story in many a boardroom!

Conflict, as opposed to tension, must be confronted by the team leader. Not to do so will lead to a loss of the leader's authority and to team effectiveness. In principle:

> **Conflict, as opposed to tension, must be confronted by the team leader.**

- the issue should be brought into the open and not avoided;
- it must be tackled with the individual/individuals concerned in a sensitive way. They may not be aware that there is a problem! Sometimes, it is necessary to tackle it on a group basis;
- the cause should be identified;
- there must be agreement on the way ahead.

Those who choose to ignore the problem in the hope that it will go away will seldom find that it does. Getting rid of the problem by having a person removed might just be putting the problem on to someone else, although it is an option that might be necessary as a last resort. Let it not be assumed, however, that conflict is easy to deal with; often it is not, although the prospect is usually worse than the confrontation itself. But it does require a degree of moral courage.

REVIEWING TEAMS

In reality most teams will fall somewhere between the two

extremes, and the performance of most teams leaves room for some improvement. One of the characteristics we noted of the effective team is that it regularly and openly reviews its performance against its task and goals, not least because no situation is ever static and no two situations are ever the same. The extent to which such an exercise is carried out, and its effectiveness, depends on the team leader. It requires confidence, maturity, and sensitive handling. Sadly, it is an exercise that is often avoided or skated over.

Some organizations are now persuaded of the value of carrying out team audits, using an external agency or person as facilitator. This may be a sensible way to introduce the concept of performance evaluation in organizations where such an activity has never been part of the culture, and indeed it is occasionally useful to have an external view. But the aim should be for reviews to be conducted by the team itself under its own leader. This means that the emphasis should be on developing the leader in such a way that he or she can carry out that function. What is encouraging is the way some senior teams now go into "retreat" for that purpose. What is sad is that the vast majority do not see the need for such an activity (or perhaps more accurately in some cases, the leader does not accept the need).

For any review to be effective (and this applies at any level), there are a number of guidelines to be followed:

- the review must be handled positively. The aim should be to look forward, learning from the experience of the past. "How might we do it better in future?" might be the theme;

- it should be objective and avoid focussing on individuals;

- it should be open and frank, and issues should not be avoided. Both good and bad points need to be addressed;

- the team leader must control but not dominate;

- points for action or further consideration must be agreed;

- some decisions can be made on the spot. Other points may

have wider implications that require further thought or consultation.

TEAMBUILDING

Most leaders are faced at some stage with having to build or rebuild a team. This might be for several reasons.

- The most obvious one perhaps is when a team has been newly established and is in the "forming" phase. A new project team is an example, especially when the individual members do not know one another's strengths and weaknesses and capabilities and there is a need to bond the team together.

- Another instance is when a team has undergone a number of changes and needs to re–establish itself. Even small changes of personnel can affect a team, especially if the "old" team had been together for a long time.

- A third example is when a team is underperforming and there is a need to build up its confidence and group identity. The need might arise or be proved as a result of a team audit or informal review: alternatively the team leader, or his or her superior, may identify the need.

Even high performance teams sometimes need to undergo a period of teambuilding. The teambuilding process may take the form of a specific "event." Many companies arrange to send teams away for a short period as part of a program to improve teamworking within Total Quality Management. More often it will be seen as part of a leader's everyday work and something that will be achieved over a considerable period of time. The way it is

> **Even high performance teams sometimes need to undergo a period of teambuilding.**

achieved will depend on the identified needs and other factors (such as time and resources), but there are a number of guidelines that bring together several of the points already discussed.

- It is important to accept and value the identity and contributions made by all individual team members. Strive to emphasize their interdependence.
- Identify the strengths and weaknesses of the team and its individual members, endeavor to capitalize on the strengths and develop in areas of weakness.
- A team exists for a purpose, not in its own right (an obvious statement, but one that needs to be made in that this fact is sometimes forgotten). Focus the team on its aims and goals and endeavor to convince members of the value of aligning individual with corporate aims.
- Be open. Admit problems and errors and review performance honestly.
- Encourage consultation in the decision–making process, be positive in making decisions and giving direction, and explain decisions.
- Build up belief in the team and mutual trust.
- Celebrate or mark in some way successes gained.
- Give credit where it is due.

There are occasions when a specific teambuilding "event" is seen as being necessary or desirable. It might consist of an extended "in–house" project or performance review. There are advantages in taking the team away to a "neutral" location for this. Most teambuilding events include a social dimension: after all less than 25 per cent of one's time is spent at work, and it is important that team members know one another in the round. In some instances a confidence-building challenge or bonding exercise might be included, preferably again in "neutral" circumstances – it is important particularly that underperforming teams get into a winning frame of mind.

Ideas for teambuilding events

Here are some "events" that organizations have used as part of teambuilding:

- awaydays and weekends for directors and senior executives (which include both business and social elements);
- formal in–company dinners;
- sponsoring or taking part in a charity event;
- entering a team for a local Fun Run;
- taking part in an intercompany "Best Business Team" competition;
- spending a weekend together in an environment that requires good teamworking and that is "neutral ground" so far as work is concerned (i.e. crewing a boat, potholing, or an "Executive Stretch" weekend);
- involvement in a local worthwhile cause over a prolonged period of time.

Performance check 3

TEAM AUDIT

1 Review the size of your team. Is it too large/small?

2 Is the team well balanced in terms of personality, expertise and experience?

3 If you have freedom of choice, do you have a satisfactory system for selecting new team members?

4 Is there division or conflict within the team? If so, what are the causes, and what have you done about them?

5 Does the team regularly review its performance, in an open and honest manner? Is such communication meaningful?

6 Could relationships with other teams be improved?

7 Do team members relate well to one another as individuals? Is there a social as well as a work dimension to the team's life and is it real or contrived?

8 Are you content generally with the overall performance of the team? Would it benefit from positive team building?

Chapter 7

◆

CROSS-CULTURAL LEADING

"Culture. The integrated pattern of human behaviour that includes thought, speech, actions and artifacts and depends on man's capacity for learning and transmitting knowledge to succeeding generations."

Oxford English Dictionary

IMPACT OF CULTURE

The reader will recall that one of the main influences affecting the way leadership is practised is culture. It can have a marked impact particularly on the style of leadership likely to be most effective. We believe there is a link, sometimes very strong, between what can be termed "social culture" (national, regional and gender) and "working culture" (professional and organizational).

Insensitivity to cultural differences, whether personal or institutional, can be a major barrier to effective working relationships. At the higher levels it may also have political and commercial implications. Sadly, a lack of

> **Insensitivity to cultural differences, whether personal or institutional, can be a major barrier to effective working relationships.**

appreciation of cultural differences and their importance is an all too common occurrence.

At corporate level, one is often struck by the failure of companies who are successful in one country or culture to operate successfully in another, and particularly by the "leadership" mistakes they make when encountering problems that have a strong local element.

X and Y Ltd, a UK pharmaceutical company, was taken over by a large US group, which tried to impose its own leadership style, strongly influenced by US culture, on its new acquisition. It was a failure, with a serious effect on morale and effectiveness. The company has since been sold again to a European group. We await to see whether the lessons have been learnt!

There has also been a relative lack of success in cross-national ventures, especially in large defence-related projects, and within national cultures, in the field of mergers and takeovers, when company cultures have clashed.

At the personal level, and as we have indicated earlier, there have been numerous examples of individuals who were successful in one culture failing to gain equal success when transplanted to another, not least when transplanted from public to private sector and vice versa.

At the other end of the spectrum are those companies and individuals that have learnt to operate successfully in other cultures. Very obvious examples are to be found among the Japanese companies operating successfully in the UK. Contrary to popular belief they have not tried to impose Japanese culture on their UK workforces, but have introduced and adapted their organizational philosophy and working practices within the British and British institutional cultures. Similarly, the most successful mergers have been amongst those companies that, rather than impose the particular culture of one partner, have sought to develop a new ethos – "vive la différence."

Cultural success?

"When dealing with businessmen of different cultures, you must show that you respect their culture – and really mean it. Then they are likely to respect yours.

Philip Horton, Chairman, Dewramet

"As an organisation we have had to go for sustained growth which we have done either by acquisition or organically by setting up new companies ourselves. We have been very influenced in the way we have done this by the experience of other groups, much of it bad experience. If we take over a company in the UK we do not force our own culture on it, especially if it is operating successfully. We allow it to keep its own, trying to influence it gradually in those areas in which changes are seen to be desirable.

On the Continent we have steered a very different course to many others. Having seen how some very successful British companies have failed to make significant headway in those different cultures – including in joint ventures – we have gone for local management of a local workforce with fairly limited central control. In the US on the other hand, where we found a business culture very alien to our own, we felt we had to put in our own people whom we could trust. But, frankly, even then it hasn't been a great success."

Senior Director, UK plc operating in service field

INTERCULTURAL WORKING

Making allowance for cultural influences becomes more difficult, often much more so, when a team contains members from several different cultural backgrounds, such as may occur in an international board or management team, a joint venture operation, or even a multidisciplinary project team. The record of working in a multicultural environment is not a particularly good one: indeed it is one of the least understood and explored areas of leadership and teamworking. There is much room for improvement in spite of the fact that we are in the age of the international market place and the international organization. Increasing collaboration between organizations and disciplines has a long way to go.

> *"I do not believe the true international company yet exists."*
>
> **Sir John Harvey-Jones**

It is sometimes wrongly assumed that because people speak the same language, or have similar professional backgrounds they will react in a similar way. Often it could not be further from the truth, as those who have been involved in Anglo-American dealings have sometimes discover: the adage "divided by a common language" is all too frequently proved to be true. The fact that English is becoming increasingly the international language increases the scope for misunderstanding.

Divided by a common language.

The strongest cultural influence is undoubtedly national or regional. People are most influenced by their home and school backgrounds, (the most formative and impressionable phase for most people probably being between the ages 10 and 18).

National and regional characteristics come to the fore particularly when pressure is on, and strongly influence individual behavior. The major areas of cultural difference appear to be in:

- *The way in which people think.*

- *The way in which they behave, including the use of body language.* Latin excitability, for example, often appears incompatible with Nordic phlegm or a quiet leadership style, and vice versa.

- *Social behavior and custom, including the influence of religion.* To err in this area can cause enormous offence particularly in Middle Eastern and Oriental countries, and in a commercial sense lead to loss of business.

- *Reaction to change and potential disorder.* Some nationalities (and institutions) appear to be more comfortable when matters are well ordered, others appear more comfortable with change. To some extent this reflects attitudes to bureaucracy.

- *Attitudes to authority.* This varies from marked deference to authority and position and a preference for a directive and perhaps formal style of leadership to an expectation and perhaps insistence on widespread consultation and discussion over decision-making.

- *Attitudes to teamworking.* This appears to be more positive in countries such as Japan than in those that place strong emphasis on the individual, although certainly in the commercial field attitudes in the latter are changing – perhaps the influence of Japanese commercial success.

- *Response to leader personality.* In countries such as the USA there is a general acceptance of the cult of leadership personality. In others there is a preference for a more self-effacing approach. This obviously has a marked influence on leadership style.

- *Work ethic.* The prevailing work culture.

- *Attitudes to the organization.* Identification with the company or organization tends to be stronger in cultures such as those in Japan and Korea, where the company or organization generally adopts a more paternalistic approach, and indeed often provides benefits that in other countries would be the responsibility of the state. It used to be a stronger influence elsewhere, but social and industrial change have weakened its effect, except perhaps in certain multinational companies that have promoted heavily corporate identification. IBM comes to mind as one company in this category, although even here there appears to have been a weakening of influence.

- *Openness to criticism.* The oriental culture is much concerned with face and affected by its loss; the North European expects and accepts public criticism more readily.

- *Values and ethics generally.* Emphasis is being placed increasingly in some Western countries on ethics, and on living values. But values differ greatly, especially in the field of commerce, and cannot really be imposed by one country on another, no matter how desirable that may seem.

- *Sexual attitudes.* These vary from the extremely macho or acceptance of the predominant role of men, to the open and egalitarian.

- *Humor.* What is funny in one culture may be offensive in another!

Attempts have been made by some to place countries into cultural groupings, which can be helpful generally. For instance, the social psychologist Geert Hofstede (using his experience with IBM as a basis) suggests eight:

- The more developed Latin (e.g. Belgium, France, Spain, Brazil, Argentina).

- The less developed Latin (e.g. Mexico, Colombia, Portugal, Chile, Peru).

- The more developed Asian (e.g. Japan, Korea).

- The less developed Asian (e.g. Pakistan, India, Taiwan, Philippines, Thailand).

- Near Eastern (e.g. Greece, Turkey, Iran).

- Germanic (e.g. Austria, Switzerland, Germany, Israel).

- Anglo (e.g. Australia, Canada, Britain, New Zealand, USA, South Africa).

- Nordic (e.g. Denmark, Norway, Sweden, Finland, Netherlands).

There are in fact a number of possible permutations, and possible additions, for example Arab. Moreover, and to reinforce a point made earlier, it could be argued that there is a well defined North American culture, and a North European culture that embraces Britain, Netherlands, Denmark and Norway. And there are the East Europeans!

MULTINATIONAL WORKING

Large multinational companies often endeavor to sublimate cultural differences and variations by developing a strong corporate ethos. IBM has already been quoted, and the MacDonald fast food chain is another that comes to mind. Arguably, however, they are never able to counter fully the stronger national cultural influence – and perhaps are best advised not to do so. Value systems particularly can be difficult to export. A system adopted over the years by some multinationals offers perhaps greater effect: the exposure of

Value systems particularly can be difficult to export.

managers to working within other national cultures and through them promoting a less intensively focussed organizational culture.

How the military learnt

One of the best and most successful examples of multicultural working comes from the military field where for generations regiments composed of soldiers of other nations were integrated generally into the British military system without loss of national cultural identity, led often by British officers on secondment. The Gurkhas are a good example of this. Perhaps the British learned valuable lessons from the intercultural explosion that led to the Indian Mutiny!

More recently, and on a much larger scale, the Gulf War showed how armies of different nations can work together successfully under great pressure, by acknowledging, accepting and not undermining the national cultures of the various contingents.

INTERORGANIZATIONAL WORKING

What can be quite surprising are the cultural differences between organizations operating in the same discipline or commercial field. This may be a result of different structures (hierarchical, matrix), size or personalities.

What can be quite surprising are the cultural differences between organizations operating in the same discipline or commercial field.

90

We watched how a joint venture was formed between three civil engineering companies to build the new Falklands airport, one of the largest projects involving British companies outside the UK in recent years. The culture in each of the companies was entirely different, to the extent that they were almost incompatible. Ultimate success was built on creating an entirely new culture that bonded the employees of all three companies together – a culture that we can still recognize and has an influence on the individuals concerned to this day.

THE PROJECT TEAM

The project team (multidisciplinary, multinational, multilevel) may pose a lesser challenge to the leader, in that it is normally set up to achieve a clearly defined objective within a given time-frame. This usually ensures that differences are minimized and subordinated to the task. The difficulties arise when the team's members are not committed full time to the task or have competing interests.

BREAKING DOWN BARRIERS

One of the main reasons for what is essentially a form of parochialism is the narrowness of individuals' cultural backgrounds, exacerbated by the inward looking nature of many organizations and commercial sectors. Hopefully that is now changing, as a new generation takes charge which has been much more widely exposed to other cultures in an age of widespread television, mass travel, educational exchange, and multitrack careers. Some of the larger companies too have a positive policy of exposing their executives, particularly during their formative years, to other cultures, through allocation and secondment. Such a policy has much to recommend it, especially when it involves living as well as working in a different culture.

Intercultural exchanges

Some parts of the British Civil Service have derived considerable benefit from arranging attachments for executive grades with industry and other organizations such as the Armed Services. There is a move now to expand the program.

The British Army has had a scheme for year-long exchanges with industry. IBM, for example, accepted a senior major into a managerial position, and a senior IBM executive became the second–in–command of an infantry battalion.

The French, of course, have a well-developed tradition of regular transfers between public and private sectors – something other countries could do well to emulate.

GETTING IT RIGHT

For those faced with leading teams whose members are drawn from one or more cultures different from their own the challenge is an interesting one, but not unsurmountable given a little thought and common sense:

- Be aware of the cultural differences and ensure that the other team members are equally alert to them. Observe and listen, learn, check.

- Respect the differences, and try to avoid imposing your own culture.

- Develop a group cultural dimension and place particular emphasis on teambuilding. Give increased importance to developing personal and social relationships.

- In the process of respecting cultural differences, avoid opting out of leadership – which can be a great temptation, especially in noncommercial organizations. People still need leadership.

- Remember that fundamentally human needs are the same, regardless of background.

As Charles Hampden–Turner, well known in Britain and the USA as a business strategist, has said: "Culture is based on communication and learning." Leaders have the prime responsibility for both in any organization.

Part III

LEADING MORE EFFECTIVELY

"People may be appointed to
positions that include a leadership
role, but they cannot be
considered to be leaders until
they have been accepted as
such by their followers."

Chapter 8

◆

TOWARD BETTER LEADERS

HIGHLIGHTING THE WAY

We have indicated already a number of ways in which individuals can improve as leaders generally: by understanding the role of the leader, the attributes required of successful leaders, the environment in which leaders have to operate, how people are motivated, and leadership within the context of the team. In this chapter, we want to look at a number of specific areas, some related to attitude, some to skills, and in all of which anyone can improve his or her performance and thus their effectiveness as leaders.

ACCEPTING THE ROLE

"People may be appointed to positions that include a leadership role, but they cannot be considered to be leaders until they have been accepted as such by their followers." This was the feeling expressed by one writer. "Granted legitimacy by followers" was suggested by another. The problem is that many who are appointed to positions of authority do not understand what their leadership function is or what it entails. Nor is it spelt out in job descriptions or personal contracts. So it often goes by default.

Because the function is so unspecific, some feel unable or unwilling to allocate time and effort to it or give it any priority. Moreover, its effectiveness is difficult to measure. What are its tangible or quantifiable results (compared say with juggling with financial assets)? There are of course no neat or easy answers to some of the questions posed (often by people to themselves).

ALLOCATING THE TIME

The allocation of time and effort to the leadership task is crucial for anyone seeking to be an effective leader. How much time and effort? This is difficult to say, other than a great deal.

The allocation of time and effort to the leadership task is crucial for anyone seeking to be an effective leader.

Making sense of time

"I estimate that I spend up to 1/3 of my time – formally unprogrammed time – on what I believe is part of my leadership role. I get out of my office, drop in on people. Chat informally, listen, and sense what is going on. It is also my most important creative time, when I have my best ideas."

Company Chairman

"A busy man always has time to do everything."

A public school Headmaster

98

> *"Those who make the worst use of their time are the first to complain of its brevity."*
>
> **La Bruyère**
>
> And on the downside,
>
> *"Work expands to fill the time available for its completion."*
>
> **C. Northcote Parkinson in *Parkinson's Law***

When time is at a premium and there is considerable pressure on the individual to do other things, it can take a lot of willpower to leave diary time free. People are often embarrassed or uncomfortable to be "unprogrammed" for any length of time. But that is what it requires. Thinking and informal communicating time are part of work, not a luxury or something accidental. It is important not to confuse the busy-ness of one's diary with efficiency and effectiveness, or urgency with importance.

It is amazing in fact how many people in senior appointments are controlled by their diaries (which usually means they are secretary controlled). This is particular noticeable in the public sector, but can also be found in the private.

Time is a precious commodity, and once spent cannot be replaced. Napoleon has been quoted as having said, "Ask me for anything but time." It requires discipline, planning, and the development of a true sense of priorities. Not to have sufficient time puts pressure not only one oneself but also on others.

Time is a precious commodity, and once spent cannot be replaced.

Principles of better time management

- Develop a personal sense of time
- Identify long-term goals
- Make middle-term plans
- Plan the day
- Make best use of your best time

Professor John Adair, *How to Manage Your Time* (1987)

Accessibility

Just as your secretary's pressure to fill the diary with meetings and appointments must be resisted, so must attempts by secretaries to isolate the busy executive – the closed door policy. There is nothing more irritating or frustrating than being forbidden access, an experience encountered often even at quite a low level. To be told by the outer office that you cannot be seen for just two minutes until at least next week (or even in the more distant future) makes the enquirer, who may require a simple but urgent

There is nothing more irritating or frustrating than being forbidden access.

decision to be made, despair of the system – and the leader. But this situation often arises. Many effective leaders counter this bureaucratic tendency (for this is essentially what it is) by having an "open door" policy. Some go further and have an open office.

> The SERCO Group has written into its charter and widely publicized a right of access by any employee to the Chairman. The Chairman himself holds open forum regularly with employees at all levels who are encouraged to question him on any aspect of the Company's operations.
>
> Tom Farmer of KWIK-FIT openly stresses his accessibility to any customer or employee.

There are obviously times when accessibility must be guarded for practical purposes (not as a routine defence mechanism), but these must be limited and strictly controlled. The applicant must always feel that his or her contribution is important and fully welcomed.

Removing interpersonal barriers

Operating an open door policy undoubtedly removes physical barriers between leader and led, but there is also a need to remove psychological barriers. One way of doing so is this. There is a tendency in most organizations for the 'led' to be summoned to the presence of the leader. This is inevitable on some occasions, and indeed sometimes desirable. More often however it is just as easy and certainly more effective to reverse the process and follow General Montgomery's rule: that visitors go forwards (or downwards in this case) not backwards or upwards. It removes an unnecessary barrier in that the subordinate will be more at ease in his or her own surrounds than in those of the superior. The

Operating an open door policy undoubtedly removes physical barriers between leader and led, but there is also a need to remove psychological barriers.

reverse does not apply. It also has the added advantage of the leader getting out and about.

"In 17 years the vice-chancellor has not once visited me in my office, or even my department."

University Department Head

To be able to 'drop in' unannounced on a subordinate and to be welcomed in doing so and to not cause stress or suspicion is the ideal interpersonal relationship to be striven for: it leads to openness, increased cooperation and better understanding. It is common practice in smaller organizations. But it may require a cultural change for it to be welcomed within the larger organization: it can cause suspicion of motives and fear of snooping, if the pervading culture is not accustomed to it. It requires considerable reassurance that you are not trying "to find them out", which takes time. Similarly it takes time to gain subordinates' trust that they can come to you with problems if the culture is an unforgiving one. They need to be persuaded that you may have faced similar problems yourself and can give them the benefit of your experience, that you really want to help them, that a problem shared is a problem halved, and that they will not be "marked down" for approaching you.

Experience has shown that it is not always to create such relationships.

Reducing barriers

As a leader

As a leader, do not use the trappings of your office to protect yourself. Think person-to-person. Encourage naturalness as the best type of dignity. Avoid role play or else it will take over and diminish your natural personality. Put your subordinates at ease so that you truly increase their dignity both in your eyes and in their own.

You cannot be a good leader unless you respect your team members. More often than not you should respect them more than feel you need to respect yourself. Your own self-respect can only come through a natural process, it cannot be captured. You can develop self-respect in subordinates.

As a subordinate

As a subordinate, do not be cowed by the trappings of the surroundings. Think person to person. Behave naturally and avoid role play – it is an unnecessary part of your defence mechanism. Put your superior at ease, so that you are no threat to his dignity and, somehow, put across that your dignity is of equal importance. Give respect as naturally as possible. The leader may have (acute) difficulties with circumstances, events, people. You can help the leader more often than you recognize.

ON PERSONALITY

There is an enduring image of the leader as an extrovert: the outgoing, hail-fellow-well-met person, brimming with self confidence, good at games, perhaps physically imposing. It stems partly from childhood memories of the type encouraged in the schools and literature when we were young, partly from the cultivation of personality by the media. Because they do not fit this image some people are inclined to shy away from a leadership role for which they may be well suited.

It is not necessary to be an extrovert to be an effective leader

> **It is not necessary to be an extrovert to be an effective leader. Indeed many of the most successful leaders have tended towards introversion.**

(this does not mean of course that extroverts cannot be good leaders). Indeed many of the most successful leaders have tended towards introversion. They have been able, however, to impress their personality on others through personal qualities such as honesty, sincerity and integrity, professional competence, their understanding of people and their development of leadership skills such as communication. In fact through having and using just those attributes listed earlier in the book.

Self-effacing leader

He did not stand out in a crowd or even draw attention to himself socially. He was a quietly spoken unassuming man who seldom offered his views in public, preferring to listen to others. He appeared very self-sufficient and took great pleasure from his cultural interests. Yet he was one of the best and toughest leaders in the business. Put him in charge of an operation, his quiet determination, his steely will, his ability to inspire loyalty, the strength and depth of his character, his integrity, all came to the fore. His team produced the best results.

Description of a distinguished SAS commander

To try to be what you are obviously not – the introvert trying to project him or herself as an extrovert – is almost always doomed to failure: to others it will appear synthetic. Personality develops with age and experience. Leadership development ideally runs parallel to personality development.

LEADERSHIP STYLE

To an extent, style reflects the personality of the leader. More importantly, it should also reflect the personality of the led, both individually and collectively. Unfortunately, style often seems to be associated with professional background, for example the military or the academic, heavily influenced sometimes by media portrayal. It is a truism, however, that those who adopt or assume such "caricature" styles are usually not particularly successful, even in their own professional surroundings.

Stereotyping

Association of style with particular groups also works to the disadvantage of those in them: the general assumption is made that all Service Officers are pompous "blimps," that academics are unworldly and incapable of making decisions, that trade unionists are confrontationalist and Luddite in their attitude to change.

Leadership has been described as "theater," and so to an extent it is. By this is meant that an effective leader can adapt his or her style to the circumstances. This requires sensitivity, forethought and a leadership attribute mentioned earlier: an understanding of people.

Leadership must always be completely sincere.

Adapting style

"Looking back on it, I had to adapt my style not only to each individual member of my management team but also to each group: the management team, the junior management teams, the assembled workforce, etc. I also had to change my general style as the organisation developed

105

from one in crisis to a mature operation. As far as my management team were concerned:

- *A lacked confidence in himself and was near to breakdown. He had to be coaxed along and his confidence built up.*

- *B was full of confidence to the point of arrogance and would argue every point. He had to be given tight guidelines initially. But he learnt quickly and I was then able to give him his head.*

- *C was stolid, unimaginative but dependable. I could give him a clear set of instructions and then leave him safe in the knowledge that they would be carried out.*

- *D needed minimum guidance. He sensed what was needed and what I required and got on with it. He just required a touch of the tiller now and then!"*

Company chief executive

ATTITUDES TOWARD PEOPLE

Effective leadership and teamworking is based on a respect for others and a true appreciation of their worth and contribution, points we have already made. Lack of respect and appreciation of others normally reveals itself and leads rapidly to a loss of group effectiveness, which in turn affects the performance of the leader. It may perhaps not be necessary to go beyond that: we may have encountered reasonably effective leaders who have a personal antipathy toward individual members of their team or organization but who nevertheless respect them, and who are able to suborn their personal feelings toward them.

In Chapter 3 we raised the question of whether it was necessary for effective leaders to like people. In many, and perhaps a majority of cases, the leader comes to like those whom he or she leads, collectively or individually. As is the case with affection toward the leader, this may be born out of respect. Arguably leaders can like individuals within the team overmuch, which can blind them to their faults, or make it particularly difficult to make certain decisions affecting them. Experience shows there can be a particular problem when working with friends.

"As a golden rule I never set out to work with friends, but I make friends of people with whom I work."

Attitudes to people – Theory X and Theory Y

Douglas McGregor in his book *Leadership and Motivation* suggests that there is an underlying assumption in many organizations that the average person is by nature indolent, lacking in ambition, indifferent to organizational needs, and by nature resistant to change. This is reflected in their structures, policies and practices (Theory X).

He rejects this approach as being based on mistaken notions, and suggests that a different attitude is required based on a more accurate assessment of human nature and motivation, that people are not by nature passive or resistant to organizational needs, that the motivation, the potential for development, the readiness to direct behavior toward organizational goals are all present in people, and that the essential task of management is to arrange organizational conditions and methods of operation so that the people can achieve their own goals best by directing their own efforts toward organizational objectives (Theory Y).

COMMUNICATION

The importance of communication in leadership has been mentioned a number of times already, and many organizations have linked communication and leadership together as providing the keystones to success. Communication is how you express and exert leadership. Without good communication the effect of potentially good leadership is negated. In the worst cases it can have serious consequences.

> **Without good communication the effect of potentially good leadership is negated.**

The penalty

You must invest time in communication. You waste time following up errors caused by a failure to communicate.

Word got out that the Company's bankers were having a long session in secret with the Board. This was interpreted by pessimists to mean that the banks were foreclosing on the Company – there had been rumors to this effect. This caused considerable unrest on the shopfloor and a temporary cessation of work. The shopfloor managers were none the wiser. In fact, the hard times were over and the Board were discussing finance for an expansion. The unnecessary cost in time and disruption.

Too often communication is interpreted only in terms of giving out information, and people are accredited as being "good communicators" when what really is being described is their oral or written articulateness. Obviously being articulate helps, and being unable to articulate one's ideas and thoughts can be a serious hindrance, although most people through practice and application can become competent in this field. Just as importantly it should embrace the receiving of information. It is always a two-way process.

The effectiveness of outgoing information should be judged by the results it produces, not by the fluency of the messenger. It is surprising how often the wrong interpretation can be put onto a message or action; therefore it is important to check that the contents have been correctly received. The message can also be distorted (either wittingly or unwittingly) by intermediaries. To ensure this is not happening it is necessary on occasion to bypass the intermediate levels which can be done even in a hierarchically structured organization without undermining anyone's authority. This is essential when the message is all important, in which case anyway it would be expected (but often does not happen). We have all played the whispering game as children and laughed at the distortion that ensues, but it often happens for real.

> **The effectiveness of outgoing information should be judged by the results it produces, not by the fluency of the messenger.**

Obviously oral communication is potentially the most effective medium to use. Sadly, it is a medium that is often avoided, not least because people lack confidence and particularly because they fear speaking formally. In the latter case, however, there are few who are not capable of doing so, with reasonable effectiveness following a little forethought and practice. It can be a daunting experience even for the most hardy, especially if the message contains unwelcome news, and if the speaker does not know the audience well. The audience however is usually more interested in the message than the messenger, and generally appreciates a face-to-face contact and honesty, more than articulateness or the use of other media.

> *"I was given notice of my redundancy by fax. I couldn't believe that after all the years I'd worked for the firm they didn't even have the guts to tell me to my face."*
>
> **A middle manager**

> *"The first I knew that I was not being retained by the firm after my articles was a note pinned to the board."*
>
> **A junior solicitor**

The real test of the effective communicator is an ability to receive information, and this appears to be the area of greatest weakness. Information is gained in a number of ways: by reading, by hearing, by seeing and by "sensing." The tendency is to rely on what from a leadership point of view are the least effective: reading, and listening to intermediaries.

By accepting the suggestion that part of the leader's job is to get out and about, the leader will inevitably hear and see things first hand – and often get a totally different impression to that given in reports. He or she is also able to get a "feel" for what is going on, the "sensing" referred to above. This is particularly important in crisis situations when the temptation is "to try and manage" the crisis from a central position which usually means being out of touch with what is really happening. But it is important on a day-to-day basis as well.

> **The real test of the effective communicator is an ability to receive information, and this appears to be the area of greatest weakness.**

Out of touch

One of the most notable aspects of the 1974 General Strike in Northern Ireland was a failure by those in authority to sense the mood on the ground at local level. The strike need never have developed but did so mainly through a failure of real communication and ultimately of leadership. The hierarchy stayed in their offices and dreamt crises which then became a reality, rather than meeting and listening to the people. "Unofficial" leadership by the militants filled the vacuum after a seemingly leaderless 48 hours, a 48 hours in which people asked endlessly: What is happening? What are they doing?

How well this might also be the case in many industrial disputes?

Experience and research show that a majority of people are not good listeners, but do not realize it. The track record among senior executives is particularly poor. Listening is a skill, and a skill that can be developed, a fact that is only now beginning to be appreciated. In the main we give ear, but do not hear. We are selective in what we hear, we are too easily distracted, and often we are preoccupied with other things.

> **In the main we give ear, but do not hear.**

Listening

"Frankly, I had never thought of listening as an important subject by itself. But now that I am aware of it, I think that perhaps 80 percent of my work depends on my listening to someone, or on someone listening to me.

"I'd been thinking about things that have gone wrong over the past couple of years, and I suddenly realized that many of the troubles have resulted from someone not hearing something, or getting it in a distorted way.

"It's interesting to me that we have considered so many facets of communication in the company, but have inadvertently overlooked listening. I've about decided that it's the most important link in the company's communications, and it's obviously also the weakest one."

Senior executive quoted in *Harvard Business Review*

Research suggests that after listening to a talk:

- we will forget between one-third and one-half within eight hours;

- we will forget 75 percent within two months.

Communication should become part of the way of life in any organization. It should be programmed in, and be both two-way and multidirectional. It is an essential ingredient of the recipe for success; and the leader should play the part of the cook. Trust people and tell them what is going on (if you don't they will guess with a 50 percent chance that they will guess wrongly), hear what they say, and watch them at work.

Communication should become part of the way of life in any organization.

"To think justly we must understand what others mean: to know the value of our thoughts, we must try their effect on other minds."

William Hazlitt

In a rare moment of revelation at the end of a seminar:

"Yes. I now recognize in what is supposed to be a two-way conversation, when I am supposed to be listening for a few moments, I am chiefly thinking about what I want to say, and looking for the earliest opportunity to butt in."

"Funny you should say that, I agree that I do just the same."

Good leaders listen.

DELEGATION

Being able to delegate has a number of advantages that are often overlooked:

- it is a great saver of that precious commodity, time;
- it enables the leader to focus on higher priority activities;
- it acts as an incentive to those given greater responsibility and can play an important part in their development. It is a good way to evaluate potential;
- it helps create a better team spirit in a group;
- it can introduce new thinking.

Some however find it difficult or are reluctant to delegate. This might be for one or a number of reasons:

- they do not know how to;
- they feel they can do the task better themselves;
- they fear loss of authority;
- their sense of security is threatened;
- they want to feel indispensable.

Increased delegation is essential if organizations are to become more efficient and management levels are to be reduced. But it requires a degree of trust, the acceptance of some risk and a permissiveness of error (although in reality this is seldom a problem area). Delegation does not of course mean abrogation of authority. Nor on the other hand should it be given in a prescriptive way, or be oversupervised.

"Tell them what you want, not how to do it, and you'll be surprised at the initiative shown."

General Patton

When delegating

- Know the person to whom you are delegating, their strengths and weaknesses.
- State how much authority you are giving and where their responsibility begins and ends.
- Give clear objectives and guidance on means and resources available.
- Give sufficient scope and incentive for use of initiative.
- Establish monitoring periods, and controls if necessary.
- Coach in times of difficulty, rather than resume control.
- Remind yourself not to interfere.
- Praise openly, but point out failings privately.

EMPOWERMENT

One of the most overused words in the 1990s has been empowerment, and with it the often associated word ownership. They are also on our list of the least understood and badly interpreted management terms. Empowerment is not about the freedom to act totally independently; it is about the acceptance of responsibility, but not the abrogation of responsibility by others. Too often, however, it is interpreted by subordinates in a self-centered and sometimes selfish way. To some it is all about taking, with little thought of giving, whereas really it is about sharing. It is about sharing information, sharing decision-making, sharing responsibility and sharing the burden. It affects structures, relationships and social processes such as communication and delegation. It is not about the privilege to act independently or in an indulgent way regardless of others. A subordinate who causes the complete failure of an enterprise by his own individual actions shows the worst aspects of misguided empowerment.

Real empowerment enhances the strength of an organization or team, and helps maximize collective and individual potential. The acid test of its effectiveness perhaps is whether a team or organization can continue to function fully in the absence of its leader(s) – an outcome weaker brethren might see as a decided threat!

Real empowerment enhances the strength of an organization or team, and helps maximize collective and individual potential.

Empowerment entails sharing in a very real way, not going through a superficial exercise. It should be an essential feature of organizations seeking to introduce flatter structures if those structures are to operate efficiently and effectively.

Not surprisingly empowerment in its true sense is resisted, especially by those who view their leadership in autocratic terms and those who fear delegation or in any way sharing authority or information. It is also resisted by those who do not want the responsibility it involves.

THE LEADER AS COACH

"Leadership is not a spectator sport ... leaders coach."
James M. Kouzes and Barry Z. Posner, *The Leadership Challenge*

One of the most important responsibilities of a leader at any level is the development of his or her team and its component members. It is however a responsibility of which many appear to be unaware or are unwilling to accept; too often it is left to others (in an organizational setting, to the personnel or training staff), or disregarded completely. Within that general responsibility is the need for personal involvement in coaching of individual members or subordinates – as is implicit in delegation, but also in a much wider sense if individual and group potential is to be realized.

Coaching

We use the word "coaching" here as opposed to mentoring or tutoring. We see a mentor as one who gives guidance, probably over a long period, to someone who seeks it, usually someone younger, more junior and less experienced. It suggests a close personal and informal relationship, normally outside any hierarchical structure, or indeed the workplace. Tutoring suggests a more formal guiding relationship between one who has particular knowledge, experience or expertise, often within a specific area or discipline, and someone whose intellectual development and understanding he or she has been given responsibility for. It is often explicitly part of a person's job. Coaching we see as being more proactive and related to short-term performance. It is an informal activity between two people, or sometimes groups, within a formal relationship structure.

Coaching requires time, patience and sympathy, but it is an investment of effort that will be repaid handsomely by its effect on performance. It is encouraging that those organizations which have focussed on quality and people are placing particular emphasis on this function of leadership, which they regard as second in importance only to the direction of whatever activity they are engaged in. If coaching is done really well, the coach should learn as much from the experience as the person coached.

> **If coaching is done really well, the coach should learn as much from the experience as the person coached.**

> *"Leaders must coach and help the development of their subordinates on a one-to-one basis: it's part of their job to improve both competence and motivation.*
>
> *"My job as a leader is to get results within the code of values I set for myself. Good leaders who coach create such a culture and environment – consciously. If done well then others will follow willingly."*
>
> **Mark Morpurgo, Chief Aide to Chairman**

Who coaches the leaders? In a hierarchy with a number of levels of leader, each is responsible for coaching the next subordinate leader, and so on. Who coaches the top leader? That is a question we shall address in Chapter 11.

How often?

"I don't want to sound sentimental," said an executive in the middle of a small dinner party. "I owe everything I've achieved to –" and he looked towards and named the host. Momentary embarrassed silence by the assembled party. It was nevertheless true. The mentoring had been over a ten-year period and the executive had passed through very

stringent and wholly objective career tests – without any strings being pulled.

"In my whole career I can only recall one person who went out of his way to coach me. If he felt that I was unsure in any way of the task he had given me, he would say 'Sit down and I will show you.' I so appreciated this, and learnt so much from it, that I always tried to follow his example. Too often I came across the opposite: someone who expected me to do everything and anything without guidance, and then react strongly if the product was not up to the standard required."

An executive's reflections

"Overmanning was obvious in our top heavy organisation. I shared an office with my boss. He tried hard to coach me, but his manner was old fashioned and patronising. My unease clearly irritated him. I was therefore uncooperative. What was worse was that neither of us were big enough men to form up to our superiors and admit that we didn't have real jobs in the first place."

Senior executive reflects

"'In your new job I shall back you up a hundred per cent with outsiders. But if you go wrong I shall tell you privately exactly what I think about you.' On that basis we got on famously and our organisation performed well."

One of the authors meets his new boss (1973)

The area of development is a broad as well as an important one, and is discussed in more detail in Chapter 11. The point being made here is that effective leaders are also effective coaches.

ATTITUDE TO CHANGE

Leadership is associated closely with change. Arguably, without change, the need for leadership is considerably diminished. We live however in a time of rapid and increasing change that affects all walks of life. Yet those in positions of authority are often curiously resistant to it. It is perhaps because they feel threatened by the uncertainty which change suggests. Certainly it challenges complacency, and it can be uncomfortable.

An effective leader is not just a passive witness to change: he or she will accept that some change is inevitable. Life cannot stand still. It is part of the leader's role to manage that change and persuade others of its benefits. Even more importantly the leader should anticipate change and initiate it where necessary. Merely reacting to changing circumstances may be too late. This is not to suggest that change is always necessary, acceptable, desirable or beneficial. Far from it. What is suggested is that the attitude to it should be positive, not negative. No organization or system exists that cannot benefit from some change.

The leader should anticipate change and initiate it where necessary.

Resistance to change is more prevalent among those in the middle ranks of the leadership structure: the "reflective layer" as described by one chief executive, the "soggy middle" by another. The inference is the same. Those in the middle of the structure are often in the most difficult position, and tend to feel more threatened. This is understandable, but not acceptable. They have to be persuaded otherwise, although if their jobs are perceived to be at risk – which is often the case nowadays – the difficulties can be considerable.

The best ideas for change often stem from below – the beneficial product of a change culture.

119

Change is often more acceptable at the lower levels where its benefits are seen more clearly. Indeed the best ideas for change often stem from below – the beneficial product of a change culture. But how many organizations enable such ideas to come forth?

Encouraging change

A hallmark of a confident and well-led organization is its willingness to invite and discuss ideas for change. But how many organizations have credible suggestion schemes (adequately rewarded), stakeholder circles (for example, UNIPART) and effective process reviews? Too often change is introduced from the top without adequate consultation or thinking through of the consequences, or without being "sold," or indeed without presenting the problems faced that might necessitate change and inviting solutions from those most affected. Not only is this bad leadership, but it is also inefficient and potentially costly.

BEING IN CHARGE

This refers not to the symbolic or representational role of the leader, important though that may be, but to two of the fundamental attributes of the effective leader, the ability to make decisions, and the acceptance of responsibility. Teams and organizations cannot function at their best without timely decision making. The making of a decision is sometimes not easy – indeed this tends to be the case more often than not. The main problems are that the full facts pertaining to the decision are seldom available, and it is often difficult to give an accurate

In reality decisions are seldom wholly right or wholly wrong; it is more a questions of the balance of advantages.

weighting to the advantages and disadvantages of any course of action. But in reality decisions are seldom wholly right or wholly wrong; it is more a question of the balance of advantages. The important thing is to have a decision – ask anyone who has worked for a tardy decision-maker – and most of us have. There is almost always a "moment of truth".[12]

Decision-making

The British Army has a simple but effective technique for decision-making under pressure. It teaches officers to go through a mental (or written process) they call "Appreciation of the Situation" which has a laid out format:

- At the outset determine the desired outcome or objective. This is not always as easy as it seems and many get it wrong.
- Establish the factors that are likely to affect the outcome and in what way (factors such as time, space, resources).
- Draw up a list of options and evaluate each. The options generally fall out of the factors considered earlier.
- Select the best option and explain why.
- Plan how the decision is to be implemented.

This well-practiced exercise should speed up decision-making when the time factor is vital. When time is more plentiful, great care must be exercised not to "situate the appreciation" – a temptation for the less competent and conscientious.

Some leaders make decision-making more difficult for themselves by excluding others from the consideration process. Yet those excluded are often in a position to provide information and expertise that could affect vitally the quality of the decision. In a majority of cases, certainly in those involving major decisions, there is sufficient time to consult the other members of the team or those likely to be affected. The

Some leaders make decision-making more difficult for themselves by excluding others from the consideration process.

wider the consultation usually the better. Where leadership is shared, for example in a boardroom, this is essential (although not always seen to be so).

The leader, or where applicable the members of the leadership team, must accept responsibility for decisions made. In the latter case, it is a matter of collective responsibility even though an individual may not fully agree with it. Responsibility, of course, goes beyond just decision-making; it affects everything that a team or organization does in a collective sense.

Prisoners of doubt?

The responsibility of what happens in prisons has recently been the subject of considerable debate in the UK. The impression given by those agencies and individuals involved has been that while they accept limited responsibility for what goes on, no one has been willing to accept total responsibility at any level, although arguably a number of people are tasked (and paid) to do so. As a consequence there has been considerable passing of the proverbial buck between prison officers, prison governors, Head of the Prison Service and the Government Minister with overall responsibility for the prisons.

ATTITUDE TO RISK

Inherent in introducing change and in making decisions is a degree of risk, risk as to the consequences. In very few circumstances can these consequences be predicted fully.

Part of leadership is assessing risk, and accepting responsibility for it. With good leadership, of course, the rest of the team will happily share that responsibility. Some of those placed in positions of leadership shy away from risk.

> **Inherent in introducing change and in making decisions is a degree of risk, risk as to the consequences.**

It is too emotional a strain. In doing so they fail to appreciate the more serious consequences that might arise should these changes or decisions not be made.

Risk should not be taken foolhardily; it should be the outcome of carefully balanced judgment. Some are prone to rushing in and taking unnecessary risk, often with dire consequences.

That is not to say that there are not occasions when a high degree of risk needs to be taken, especially when the stakes are high: commercial survival, or avoidance of military defeat.

"Who dares, wins."
Motto of the British SAS Regiment

HANDLING FAILURE

Perhaps the greatest pressure on a team's cohesion and effectiveness comes from failure and with it the greatest challenge for the leader. We witness or hear of the corporate consequences of failure on an almost daily basis in such diverse areas as industry, sport, politics and war. Teams and organizations are liable to fall apart or at least seriously under-achieve. On the other hand we hear also of the opposite: leaders (and it is the leaders) who confront failure positively, learn from the experience, avoid recrimination, emerge from the experience strengthened and help their team or organization rebound to success.

Perhaps the greatest pressure on a team's cohesion and effectiveness comes from failure and with it the greatest challenge for the leader.

> *"The seemingly high performance team was completely thrown by its setback. It could not handle failure. The whole thing disintegrated. The team members blamed everything and everyone other than themselves, the captain went into his shell. They needed gripping firmly but there seemed to be no one willing to do it."*
>
> Observation on a national sports team

> *"We operate in a competitive world and most of the work we do has to be won in open competition. Inevitably, we have our failures, which come sometimes after months of hard work by a project team and considerable investment of resources. And we play to win. But we go out of our way to avoid recrimination. No one is blamed. Rather, we sit down and learn from our experience and determine how we can do it better next time."*
>
> plc Chairman

Failure can bring with it bitterness, demoralization, and criticism, particularly of the leader(ship). It can also lead in extreme cases to severe financial loss or worse, and heavy psychological pressure. It demands strong leadership therefore to turn those negative effects and reactions to positive advantage. The key elements of this are:

- to accept that the failure has occurred and not to pretend it did not happen;
- to avoid walking away from the failure;
- for the leadership to accept overall responsibility for the failure (and detailed responsibility if that is attributable to the leadership);
- to avoid unnecessary recriminations;
- to determine to learn from the experience and gain agreement how mistakes made can be avoided in the future, which may involve some reorganization, restructuring, or individual development;
- to seek to rebuild the organization's or team's confidence if this has been damaged.

Individual failure by the leader can be even more difficult to face up to, although it need not be. Sometimes it may be a failure that suggests a flaw in the personality of the leader, or in the leader's capacity to lead under particular circumstances. More often, however, it is a question of faulty judgment, or an unusual set of circumstances unlikely to recur. An admission of error or failure and a measure of humbleness can go a long way to mitigating the effect. It is surprising how quickly a leader who says "I'm sorry, it's my mistake, I got it wrong" is usually forgiven. Unfortunately, some cannot accept what they perceive would be a loss of face. In those cultures where "face" is important, the consequences of this are sometimes dire.

Mea culpa

Lord Whitelaw, when a member of the British Government, gained enormously in stature by his willingness publicly to admit having made a mistake, a rare quality in any politician. It is a pity that others do not learn from and follow his example.

In those cultures where "face" is important, individuals find it is less easy to apologize for error. An example is the difficulty Japanese political leaders experienced when pressed to apologize for their country's behavior during World War II. This does not mean necessarily that individuals do not accept having made mistakes and responsibility for the ensuing consequences. They find it hard however to suffer a perceived loss of face by admitting and having to live with the fact. This leads sometimes to extreme acts on the part of individuals against themselves, for example by committing suicide.

GRATITUDE

One of the more powerful and sincere acts of leadership and undoubtedly the easiest and least costly is the recognition of other people's efforts. Saying "thank you" or "well done" for an act or job accomplished – even though it might be part of their remit – can have a quite striking effect on people and their motivation. It is remarkable that this should be so – perhaps because it still seems to be such a rare occurrence.

> **One of the more powerful and sincere acts of leadership and undoubtedly the easiest and least costly is the recognition of other people's efforts.**

AUDITING THE LEADER'S PERFORMANCE

Increasingly, all aspects of an institution's activities are subject to audit. But who audits the leader? At the lower levels this can be done partially through an ap-praisal system, although many have a cynical disregard for the effectiveness and value of such processes. At the lower level too it can be done by line managers accepting the role of coach, a practice that is spreading. At the higher levels it is left more to the

But who audits the leader?

individual to evaluate him or herself through self-analysis, or seeking counsel from a respected and trusted friend or colleague – which often means it is avoided, sadly so as it really does diminish the potential of those individuals. The British Army has an interesting way of tackling the problem, which can become acute in a very hierarchical structure. It is accepted practice within military culture that the padre (or sometimes the medical officer) is one person who is able to approach his commander and give an honest opinion, which will be respected – although obviously not always accepted. Senior officers often seek such opinion from close aides – and get some very frank answers.

Rather like effective teams, we have noted how often really effective leaders review their own leadership performance, seldom being fully satisfied. We have noted too that poor or indifferent leaders usually avoid exposing themselves to such a challenge – an attitude that stems as much from arrogance and conceit as from lack of confidence.

Performance check 4

SPRINGBOARDS TO IMPROVEMENT

1 Are you clear what your goals are, and are they being communicated to and understood by those for whom you are responsible?

2 Is adequate direction being given to all members of the team/organization?

3 Are you impossibly short of time? If so, have you really analyzed how your time is allocated? Are you ill at ease with having free time in your day? Are you diary driven? Do you delegate sufficiently? Are you prepared to risk errors by subordinates?

4 Do you allocate any time to coaching subordinates?

5 Do you accept responsibility for subordinates' mistakes?

6 Do you **really** listen? Have you checked with others?

7 Are you accessible enough? Do you make everyone go through your outer office? Are you overprotected?

Chapter 9

♦

MORAL CHALLENGES

BROADENING THE DEBATE

In earlier chapters we have raised a number of moral issues, such as the fundamental need for integrity, personal and corporate, and a requirement for moral courage to be shown by leaders. We believe that in fact leadership nearly always has a moral component or dimension.

> **Leadership nearly always has a moral component or dimension.**

There are several aspects of a moral nature that we feel need to be addressed specifically in this chapter. They are aspects which most leaders of experience have had to consider or face up to at one time or another – and for which there are no textbook solutions!

LEADER AUTHORITY

The word "authority" sometimes causes confusion in people's minds and is often regarded as being synonymous with power. We hear of nonexecutive directors on the one hand and school prefects on the other claiming they have no authority, when what they really mean is that they lack power of direct sanction.

Authority can be derived from several sources which are not mutually exclusive:

- some authority derives from position or office, for example that held by a managing director or a headmaster;

- knowledge or expertise, for example that of a lawyer or doctor;

- a right to sanction, for example the ability to sack someone. This tends to be the source of authority most frequently used in commercial life;

- a person's character or personal attributes.

In the first three instances, the authority is invested in an individual. In the latter, it has to be earned, which makes it that much more difficult to exercise. Yet it is the main source of authority of the effective leader and is potentially the most potent. It is also the least tangible.

Challenges to leader authority

Most leaders face challenges to their authority at one time or another. It may be direct or indirect, formal or informal. It may arise for instance from a vote of no confidence, refusal to accept a decision, the overstepping of bounds or authority by a subordinate or team member, or a misdemeanor.

Most leaders face challenges to their authority at one time or another.

Some challenges to authority might be described as "trying it on" and can and must be dealt with immediately either quietly and privately or publicly as the situation demands. Other challenges are potentially more difficult to handle and more uncomfortable. Nevertheless, they must be confronted sooner rather than later if the leader is not to lose authority. Unfortunately, some challenges develop gradually, especially those within a small team, and it is difficult in the early stages to be absolutely certain that a challenge does exist and therefore to confront it.

One of the most difficult challenges Mr B faced occurred over the implementation and interpretation of a policy decision he had made in what was a particularly sensitive area. He became convinced but could not prove that the spirit if not the letter of his policy was not accepted and implemented by D. D's attitude was affecting others. Mr B eventually confronted the person concerned, who strenuously denied the allegations, but made comments that really supported Mr B's case. In the end Mr B felt that D would never accept his authority in this area, and reluctantly had to have D sent to another department.

TRUST

For a person to trust another, he or she has to know and have confidence in that person's competence, knowledge and intentions. The latter are of course difficult to determine. Everyone has their hidden side. A major challenge to any leader is gaining and maintaining the trust of those he or she leads. Trust is like a reputation: hard to earn, easy to lose, and extremely difficult to regain.

Trust is like a reputation: hard to earn, easy to lose, and extremely difficult to regain.

For one person to trust another he or she must have confidence in that person's competence or potential competence, and integrity. Part of building a team is developing that confidence between leader and members, and among the members them-selves. This requires openness and honesty, and, on occasion, a degree of moral courage on the part of the leader.

> *"Trust is the absolute key to good leadership. In a large corporation people have a lot of agendas, but loyalty must be seen to be two-way. There is no place for lies. Weaknesses can be seen. As long as people try hard you can make some allowances. It's been said to me by a Trade Union leader, 'Often we haven't liked what you've said to us or how you've said it. But we have always trusted you.' Nowadays you've got to have been seen to have reached a position of leadership on your own merits, or people won't trust you fully. Building loyalty, trust and confidence is very important and satisfying."*
>
> **Murray Easton, Chief Executive, Yarrow Shipbuilders Ltd**

LOYALTY AND THE LEADER

Perceived conflicts of loyalty rise frequently, and often present leaders with their most difficult moral challenges. Loyalty is often regarded by some as an essential quality in a leader and can easily be misunderstood or misplaced. It often is. Loyalty should be governed overall by a person's beliefs, principles and standards, and not conveniently confused with self or parochial interest. Beyond that, it is more a question of judgment than of absolutes. It should never be used as a cover-up for negligence or wrongdoing.

In practice, loyalty is often thought of as being one way, from the bottom to the top. It is expected and indeed demanded of subordinates. Loyalty from the top down is equally necessary, but sadly less common.

In a corporate sense it is not disloyal to express views on any

132

question under consideration, even though they may not coincide with those of the leader. Once a decision has been made, however, it should be supported loyally and without criticism, unless that decision involves compromising integrity or principle. As suggested in the previous chapter, few decisions are ever wholly right or wholly wrong, but more often than not based on balanced judgment.

The duty of the leader is to ensure that the interests of subordinates or the team are always honestly and fairly represented. But this should not be to the disadvantage of the organization as a whole, a mistake sometimes made by, for example, divisional managers or directors as members of a senior corporate management team.

Priorities

"The problem I am faced with on the board is the attitude of the divisional managers who constantly over-represent the interests of their own departments and fail to see that as members of the directing board their loyalty should be through that board to the company as a whole."

The chairman of a private company

The leader is also responsible for the performance of teams or subordinates and should not seek to shelter behind shortcomings or mistakes by them which are the result of his or her planning and supervision. On the other hand, subordinates who are not up to their task, or who make unacceptable mistakes, should not be overprotected.

"Loyalty, analysed, is too often a polite word for what would more accurately be described as 'a conspiracy for mutual inefficiency.'"

Sir Basil Liddell Hart

POPULARITY VERSUS RESPECT?

Although a minority of those charged with responsibility take a form of perverse pride in being unpopular most people do not: they fear not being liked. This is a normal human reaction. Anyone who wishes to be an effective leader, however, cannot at the same time try to court popularity. There will be conflict and contradiction of aims and priorities. More importantly, the leader should endeavor to earn the respect of those for whom he or she has responsibility; a respect for fairness, integrity, personal example and competence as a leader. Respect is harder to earn than popularity, but it is potentially more enduring. It can lead in time to genuine affection and per-

> **Respect is harder to earn than popularity, but it is potentially more enduring.**

haps ultimately to popularity. Seldom does it happen the other way round.

Popularity

Political leaders frequently fall into the trap of seeking approbation through proposing or introducing popular measures, which are often seen by an increasingly sophisticated (and sceptical) electorate as an attempt to buy votes. The gain is usually short-term.

> *"Popularity is a crime from the moment it is sought; it is only a virtue where men have it, whether they will or no."*
> **George Savile, *Moral Thoughts and Reflections* (1750)**
>
> *"Discuss unto me; art thou officer? Or art thou base, common and popular?"*
> **Shakespeare, *Henry V***
>
> *"We can always make ourselves liked provided we act likeably, but we cannot always be esteemed, no matter what our merits."*
> **Nicolas Malebranche (1867)**

> *"The man with a host of friends who slaps on the back everyone he meets is regarded as the friend of nobody."*
>
> **Aristotle**

Respect

Respect also instills confidence and often leads to a sense of pride in the led both in themselves and in their leader.

> *"You must earn the respect of those you work with. Know your staff. Be fair and honest and thoroughly know your business. You have to assist people to run their particular departments in the most efficient way, and get them to communicate freely and express to you openly those issues which many would prefer to hide from you.*
>
> *"You have to be positive in the handling of a board, and take action against less motivated members. No effective company can afford passengers. You cannot be everyone's friend, and their opinion of you, expressed to others, is quite meaningless or unimportant.*
>
> *"Taking on responsibility for a company that is in a bad way can be difficult, and may mean autocratic and quick-fire decision-making, as time is not on your side. However, even then, you must respect the people and the job in hand, and show them that you do so. People respect a positive decision-maker. As a consequence, you in your turn may be respected."*
>
> **Sir Robert Easton, Former Chairman, Yarrow Shipbuilders Ltd**

DREADED REDUNDANCY

Few organizations in recent years have avoided the necessity of having to declare members of staff to be redundant, either as a result of business loss, corporate financial problems, takeovers or restructuring. Breaking such news can be a painful process, and demands a degree of moral courage and sensitivity on the part of leaders – courage and sensitivity that not all show. It is important to both parties that the action is rationalized and explained face to face. But the leader's task does not end there: it is necessary for any leader worth the title to follow through the action by giving or arranging advice and help for the individuals affected. In the case of large-scale redundancies most organizations deal extremely sympathetically with individuals. But the psychological impact of job loss should not be underestimated, and while material compensation will be welcomed by all, in many instances it will never offset fully the impact of being removed from one's job.

PRIVILEGE OR PRIVILEGES

Leadership is a privilege, and not about privileges. Privileges are often bestowed on those appointed to positions of leadership, but they can be a barrier to effective leadership. Sadly, however, the focus of some individuals is on the perks rather than the responsibility, often to a ludicrous extent.

> **Leadership is a privilege, and not about privileges.**

Some privileges are understood to be part of a reward package. But often they are unnecessary, and we have been impressed by the lengths to which some organizations have gone to remove anything or any practice that can be remotely divisive in leadership terms. Gone in many instances are the executive dining rooms, toilet facilities, parking facilities and even plush offices. Introduced have been private medical treatment for all, common working hours, holiday entitlements and even dress. It usually occurs in those organizations with a strong leadership culture – and which are usually the most successful in their fields.

Chapter 10

◆

LEADERS UNDER PRESSURE

PAIN OR PLEASURE?

There are times when it is not easy or pleasurable being the leader. This is especially so when situations arise that are potentially difficult or might involve unpleasantness but nevertheless have to be confronted – and when the inclination of most people is to avoid such situations. Despite this leadership can be very satisfying and fulfilling, especially when difficult situations have been overcome successfully.

> **There are times when it is not easy or pleasurable being the leader.**

CAUSE AND EFFECT

Difficult situations may arise from a variety of circumstances such as interpersonal conflict as described earlier, out of moral issues, or be brought about by external circumstances. Whatever the cause the effect is a degree of pressure on the leader and the team – using team in the widest sense.

All pressures are stressors (i.e. are capable of causing stress).

Stress is, of course, part of everyday life, and a degree of stress is present in most team situations. Properly controlled it can be creative, but unnecessary stress should be avoided or minimized.

As individuals, we all react differently or in differing degrees to pressure generally and to different types of pressure. We may react differently to the same pressures in changed circumstances. Most of us need pressure of one sort or another to perform our best, so long as that pressure remains at a reasonable level.

DEADLINES

The most common pressure to which most individuals and teams are subjected is the deadline, the combined pressure of time, effort and resources. Many people respond well to deadlines and indeed work best to them, so long as they are realistic. It often brings out the best in us. Indeed, we sometimes impose artificial deadlines on ourselves for this reason. Most frequently, however,

The most common pressure to which most individuals and teams are subjected is the deadline.

deadlines are externally imposed, especially in the commercial field. The deadline of the tender, the impending strike, the time of the meeting, or the shipment date. Externally imposed deadlines are sometimes negotiable; often, however, they are not. Deadlines need to be controlled, and it is part of the role of the team leader, at any level, to provide that control. Improperly controlled, they can inflict serious damage on both the individual and the team.

The first reaction, especially to a sudden deadline, is often one of panic. Some, especially leaders, may rush headlong into decisions or actions. It is at this point that the firmest leadership is required in order to convert the emotion generated into constructive action. This requires:

- engaging the attention, energies and involvement of all those affected at the earliest possible time;

- a cool analysis of the implications and the requirement;

- clear and timely decision–making;

- sensible delegation and allocation of tasks;

- effective control of time and effort.

Many of these aspects were discussed in Chapter 8. The leader's role is to maximize the team's output by:

- coordinating effort;

- ensuring that focus is maintained;

- instilling confidence in individuals and in the team as a whole, coaxing and injecting a sense of urgency as required and avoiding at all costs becoming unnecessarily involved in detail which could be best left to others. The reward is in the satisfaction and sometime exhilaration of a deadline being met.

OVERCOMMITMENT

Even without specific deadlines leaders often find themselves under considerable pressure to allocate sufficient time to their various commitments.

We suggested earlier that too many executives were diary driven, and we also highlighted the benefits of delegation. For most it is also a question of prioritizing our tasks, separating the essential from the trivial, allocation and strict control of time to the essential, making greater use of delegation and empowerment, and ruthlessly pruning out the nonessential.

The problem is, that many in positions of leadership want to be involved in everything, want to feel indispensable, take a perverse pride in overcommitment, and perhaps fear delegation.

They are the ones who become highly stressed, and more likely to suffer ill health, appear often incapable of making clear decisions, and are seldom properly prepared for meetings – in other words, are less than fully effective as leaders. They complain, but the fault is nearly always their own.

> *Leadership is more difficult as you go up. Your attention span gets smaller – there is so much to think about, as well as do.*
>
> **Chairman**

UNCLEAR ROLES

People generally like to know where they stand. They need a clear idea of what their task is, and what is expected of them, what the bounds of their own and others' responsibilities are, and where authority lies. Any blurring or misunderstanding in these areas can cause considerable stress. Indeed some recent research suggests that it is the single greatest cause of stress within many organizations and teams. Yet it is surprising how often there is a failure to acknowledge this. There is a reluctance, for example, to give individuals a written task or job description or to clarify the workings of an organizational matrix structure. It can

If there is any room for doubt, seek clarification.

lead to unnecessary interpersonal and intergroup conflict, overlapping or the reverse – and it can be extremely inefficient. The pressure can be particularly acute between individual team leaders, or leaders at different levels, and quickly affects the rest of their teams. The moral is: if there is any room for doubt, seek clarification.

INSUFFICIENT OR INADEQUATE RESOURCES

A perennial problem faced by leaders and managers is a shortage of resources, financial, material or personnel, to carry out whatever task they have to undertake. Resources of all types are usually at a premium; we are seldom given an unlimited supply. In fact such a situation is probably as undesirable as it is unreal. The problem, more often than not, lies in the equitable distribution and control of resources, rather than the overall provision. There is a marked human tendency to hoard resources against possible future requirements, rather than to think in terms of current need.

Such a situation is often to be found within teams, as well as between groups. A function of the leader is to ensure an equitable share of resources both among team members, and more widely – that breadth of horizon that effective team leaders should display.

Should resources genuinely be short, it is the task of the leader to represent that situation and its possible consequences, and then to explain fully why such a request cannot be met. Most people will then accept the situation. Without adequate explanation, it can become a major source of discontent, and an easy excuse for poor performance.

FUTURE UNCERTAIN

An underlying pressure on many organizations and teams and the individuals in them is that of longer team security and survival. This affects both commercial and noncommercial organizations. It is a pressure that has increased markedly in recent years as competition has become more severe. The search has been for ever-increasing cost effectiveness and organizational structure has been under threat. The effect has perhaps been greater on those in middle or lower level leadership teams who have in the main been used to long-term security, are essentially "company men" and in many cases have become institutionalized in their thinking and attitudes. It poses one of the most difficult challenges for the team leader, whose own future may also be perceptibly less secure. It requires leadership through both organizational and cultural change.

Change and attitudes to change were discussed in Chapters 4 and 8. We stressed then that change and leadership were closely associated. Change is also associated increasingly with organizational life: without change or improvement organizations will have difficulty in surviving in today's environment. Indeed, change is necessary even to maintain a steady state. Trying to retain the status quo means, commercially, almost certain decline. The real challenge facing the leader is in persuading others that they really do have control over their own future, both individually and collectively, that the perceived threats of change are far less, and the effects far less painful than the possible alternatives. The challenge to the overall leadership is in ensuring that control over the future is a reality.

"There are three kinds of business. There are those which anticipate change, those which react to change, and those which ignore change. The first will flourish. The second will struggle to survive. And the third will not survive."
Royal Society of Arts, *Tomorrow's Company* (1995)[13]

GOOD COMPANY CULTURE

"More than ninety five per cent are decent people and want to prove themselves. I believe in integrity and try to build a high degree of trust. Proof? Forty per cent of Kwik-Fit people own shares in the company. This helps in fostering a 'can do' team culture. We have well designed 'procedures,' of course, but they have to be applied sensibly. Most of our customers are 'distress purchasers' and we genuinely try to put their minds at rest and give them really good value for money. That's much more than good management. Everyone together must want to help the customer – that's good teamwork."

Tom Farmer, Chairman, KWIK-FIT plc

A unique culture exists in every organization, in terms of its functional working practices and social life, which gives it a collective character reflecting the daily behavior of individuals. Many aspects are good and contribute to the organization's ability to deliver. Others are detrimental, such as the habit of avoiding work, coffee-housing, petty pilfering and control/accounting slackness, harassment of staff, alcoholism, etc. The corporate culture of the organization is very much the environment in which the leaders work. It is their duty to ensure as healthy a cultural environment as possible. Sometimes the working culture is so bad that only a "new broom" can change it for the better. Often this takes great leadership skills, hard work – and moral courage to tackle and transform.

OVERINTERFERENCE

One of the temptations some executives find hard to resist is to interfere with a subordinate's work, and by extension that of the subordinate's team. As often as not this stems from benevolence, rather than a conscious wish to interfere. Just as often, however, it is interpreted as a lack of confidence, and rather than helping the subordinate it may undermine his or her performance, and cause resentment and unnecessary stress. If it is a lack of confidence, this should be spelt out rather than implied. If not, then let the subordinate get on with the task – assuming, that is, that the task has been clearly outlined in a way that leaves no doubt as to the desired outcome. This is not to contradict what was suggested earlier, that the leader has a coaching role. Interfering is not coaching by another name.

> **Interfering is not coaching by another name.**

NOT UP TO THE TASK

There are occasions when a team and/or a teamleader are not up to the task required of them. It should be obvious to those at the next higher level, and will usually be sensed by the leader or the team itself (although some may be oblivious to the fact). Either way, it is a potential cause of stress, and as such needs to be addressed. Importantly, the cause or causes must be ascertained. It might be the personality of the team leader; weakness in the team's composition; or a matter of training and development. It might be a relatively minor matter. However, things cannot be left as they are; no organization can afford teams that underperform. Most frequently it is a matter of training and development, a subject addressed in the next chapter.

SACKING

There are inevitably instances when individuals have to be

removed. They have shown themselves to be incapable of change or improvement; or they are responsible for irreconcilable clashes within the team. Removal should be an action of last resort. Some unfortunately seem to take a perverse pleasure in a reputation as a "sacker" but the majority try and avoid such a situation and agonize over the making of such a decision. As in the case of redundancy, it is the duty of the immediate superior, the leader responsible, to explain the circumstances and reason for the decision face to face. It is often a difficult and painful task, but one that must not be avoided. Depending on the maturity and resilience of the person sacked, the leader should consider follow-up action to help re-establish the person elsewhere. This, however, would not be wise if the person would feel that salt is being rubbed in the wound.

It is as well to consider the decision to sack a person in the light of good leadership practice. Sometimes sacking a subordinate reflects on poor leadership rather than inefficiency or ill will of the subordinate; many a good person has been demotivated by a bad leader. Such actions are noticed by others and can confirm their suspicions that it is perhaps time that the leader himself should go.

After the deed

"Having sacked an individual for bloodymindedness, I was surprised to receive some months later a request from an employer for a reference for the same man. Admiring his nerve, I gave him an honest reference of his potential and he joined the company.

"Another ex–employee, who had to leave the organization after being awarded a three-month prison sentence following a pub brawl, found I had arranged an interview on his release. A good worker, he landed the job and I got the satisfaction of putting someone back on his feet."

Senior manager

EMOTION

Underpinning the performance of any effective leader and team is an emotional commitment. Leadership is an emotional process, and it is difficult to see how anyone who lacks emotion or feeling can be an effective leader in a free and open society or environment. Leaders must be real people with normal emotions and emotional needs. But these emotions, especially those of a negative nature, have to be contained even under severe pressure. Otherwise the leader loses not only personal control but also possibly control of the situation and the team. Uncontrolled anger, bitterness, frustration, self-pity, fear, anxiety are understandable reactions to some of the pressures outlined above, but can have a negative effect if allowed free play. They cloud judgment, undermine team confidence and cohesion, and destroy in others respect for the leader. It is also the leader's job, of course, to seek to influence emotion in others, to counter those of a negative nature, and to instill confidence, hope, enthusiasm, ambition and fellow feeling in the team's members.

Performance check 5

WHAT PRESSURES?

1 What has been the reaction in your organization to recent deadlines? Was it a controlled or uncontrolled reaction?

2 Do people have a clear idea as to their role and responsibilities? Do they have accurate and meaningful job descriptions?

3 Is performance being impeded by lack of adequate resources? Has a thorough cost/benefit analysis been done to remedy the situation?

4 Is the organization really addressing the future and anticipating change? Is everyone necessary being involved in thinking about the way ahead?

5 Are there good and sympathetic procedures for handling redundancies and removals?

6 Do senior staff enjoy privileges or perks that are unnecessary and might be seen as less than deserved and divisive?

Chapter 11

◆

SELECTING AND DEVELOPING LEADERS

A NEGLECTED AREA

One of our assumptions (and one that is increasingly accepted generally) is that most people possess an innate ability to become an effective leader, although that ability is often not obvious. The challenge we face therefore is to uncover that ability and determine its full extent and potential, as well as the circumstances in which it might be most successfully applied. In practice, sadly, the assessment of leadership potential and the selection and development of people we want to be leaders are much neglected and indeed little understood areas, even in large organizations. One of the consequences of this is that the organizations themselves often fail to realize their corporate potential. There are a number of reasons for this neglect. In particular:

- There is a widely held belief that informal and essentially subjective assessment and selection (based on "gut feeling" or general observation) is sufficient. "We know our people" is the message; how untrue this can be. All too often, of course, it leads also to corporate cloning or stereotyping and unimaginative institutional and organizational leadership.

- There is a failure to appreciate the extent to which people can and do change, for better or for worse. Personal development, personal circumstances such as marriage, experience of job achievement or failure, work environment can all have an effect. Too often, however, judgments are formed on individuals that remain unchanged over the years with the result that individuals are unfairly advantaged or disadvantaged. Both they and the organization suffer.

- Performance and experience at a lower level are (often wrongly) judged to provide sufficient indication of suitability for a higher level which again can lead to over- or under-promotion. The well-known adage that most people are promoted one level beyond their competence is too often exemplified. Unfortunately, it is not easy to prove the reverse, that individuals have been under-promoted. It is our experience that an appreciable number, who are only adequate performers at a lower level, often do better, given the opportunity, at a higher level. Outstanding performers at one level often cannot make a successful transition or perform adequately at a higher one.

- Linked to the above, there is a failure to recognize not only that the demands placed on leaders and the requirements of leadership differ according to the level, but also to the situation. The crisis usually requires a different type of leader to the steady state; the highly institutionalized organization a different type to the entrepreneurial.

The end result of all this can be inadequate performance and undue stress on the leader concerned, and frustration for other people, and of course an adverse effect on the organization.

> *"In a hierarchy every employee tends to rise to his level of incompetence."*
>
> **L. J. Peters and R. H. Hull,** *The Peter Principle*
>
> *"Comrades, you have lost a good captain to make a bad general."*
>
> **Saturninus (c 100 BC)**

> *"Smooth answers smooth the path to promotion ... more and more does the 'System' tend to promote to [positions of control], men who have shown themselves to be efficient cogs in the machine."*
>
> **Sir Basil Liddell Hart**

ASSESSING LEADERS

A need may arise for people to be assessed for their leadership potential for one or all of three reasons which may or may not be related:

1 To determine whether they are suitable for a particular appointment, career, or promotion. This is the most likely reason.

2 As an aid to identifying their personal development needs. This is unfortunately less likely.

3 To increase their self–knowledge. Such an occurrence is rare, although effective leadership is arguably based more on self–knowledge than on any single factor.

How the assessment process is carried out and how effectively is, to say the least, varied.

FORMS OF ASSESSMENT

A majority of organizations, and this includes many major companies and departments, still carry out no form of specific leadership assessment whatsoever, either formal or informal. A growing number have or are introducing an appraisal system that addresses leadership but only among other skills and attributes. A relatively small number carry out more formal assessment either in–house or using one of a number of commercially run assessment centers that have been established in recent years.

Chance selection

"We rely solely on our own judgement in making appointments. There's a 50 per cent chance we might get it right."

Chairman of a large multinational

Appraisal systems

Relying on an appraisal system is better than having no system other than personal judgment on which to depend. Indeed every organization should have an appraisal system in that it can perform a very useful function. And some organizations have introduced very comprehensive and effective schemes. There are however a number of disadvantages if they are used as the sole basis for assessment and selection:

- their effectiveness is very dependent on the skill of the appraiser both in preparing the appraisal and in conducting the appraisal interview. It is a task that few relish or conduct well;

- it is a very subjective exercise, and often resented as such by interviewees;

- interviewees tend to overfocus on the less positive aspects of the appraisal;

- appraisal systems generally are not good at identifying potential. They are about past and current performance in a particular job;

- appraisals more often than not reveal as much about the appraiser as the appraised.

Thus we believe they do serve a useful function in personnel management terms generally in that, if conducted properly, they provide a record and subjective assessment of performance, can help identify development needs, and expose the aspirations of those being appraised. Guidance on the leadership content is given at the end of this chapter.

A good appraisal system makes the appraisers think very hard not only about their subordinates but also about themselves as leaders.

> **A good appraisal system makes the appraisers think very hard not only about their subordinates but also about themselves as leaders.**

Leadership assessment programs

The value of well-designed assessment programs, whether run in-house or by independent commercial organizations, is that they are likely to be more objective (especially if those supervising the assessment do not know personally those being evaluated) and importantly to be perceived as being objective by those being assessed. It comes as a surprise in fact to many – and a relief to some – that the good scientifically based systems can produce accurate results. Whereas in the appraisal interview a comment often encountered is: "That's not me," the opposite is frequently encountered in the assessment debrief – where such a debrief is included. Unfortunately, however, a number of systems and tools are used in the assessment field that are not well validated or wholly credible: some overfocus on (historic) performance rather than on potential. Others can be manipulated by experienced participants. And many tend to look at the individual in isolation rather than in relation to the group – which is after all what leadership is about. To be truly effective, in fact, those designing programs need to use a variety of systems and tools to enable them obtain a true and rounded picture of an individual and of his or her potential. Reliance primarily on one system (for example, on one form of psychometric measurement) can result in an incomplete or distorted profile being produced.

A Start Point

The UK Armed Services pioneered leadership assessment centers in this country with the introduction in the 1940s of boards to select individuals for officer training. These were well researched scientifically, and the programs introduced then are still largely valid today – and have also been used successfully by industry and commerce. Unfortunately their value is underexploited in that

- The individual is not debriefed other than very generally and usually in pass or fail terms. This is a great pity because the individual could gain a great deal from the exercise.

- The outcome is not used as a basis for the individual's development.

The excellent rationale for the assessment unfortunately stops there; the Armed Services have not yet appreciated fully that people and circumstances change, and that assessments are usually only valid for a few years at most. No objective assessment is carried out later (other than for specialist forces). Other parts of the public sector use an extended interview process to select those for more senior rank or training but only at the higher levels. The weakness here lies in the lack of any objective system earlier on, hence only those subjectively assessed and promoted surface higher up often by chance – which must be regarded as inefficient from an organizational point of view.

One of the best known and largest commercial organizations in the assessment field is Saville & Holdsworth Ltd. The company uses a range of scientifically based tools and concepts, many developed in–house by their scientists. They offer an integrated approach based on diagnosis of organizations and jobs, assessment of individuals, their subsequent development, and performance monitoring.

No matter how good the assessment programs available, they are concerned with evaluating an individual's potential generally rather than selecting them for specific appointments. Nevertheless, formal assessments are sometimes included as part of a selection process, for a specific job, a process sometimes conducted by search agencies – a course of action not without its dangers.

The outcome of assessments, either from appraisals or formal assessment programs, cannot or should not be used as the sole means of selection. They provide guidance, sometimes extremely valuable guidance, on an individual's potential to fill a more senior appointment effectively. Usually however there are a number of environmental factors that need to be considered also and judgments made by people who have detailed personal knowledge and experience of the circumstances.

IMPORTING LEADERS

There are occasions in most organizations when a suitable leader for a particular post cannot be found from within. This happens especially at the more senior levels, or when it is felt that a complete change is needed. Resort is then usually made to the use of headhunting executive-search agencies or to open advertising, or a combination of both. While there can be great merit in following this course of action, there are inherent dangers unless great care is taken; research suggests that it has resulted in as many disastrous failures as notable successes. A 50 percent failure rate is not uncommon.

Particular care must be taken that anyone selected in this way has the potential to be effective in that particular organization and its culture, at that particular time in the prevailing circumstances and with the personalities already in place. The fact that he or she has been successful in another environment is of course a good indicator, but not necessarily more than that. And it is suggested that any shortlist should also include the best internal candidates if only as a comparator. The question should also be asked: have those already in the organization in fact been adequately or objectively evaluated. The talent may be there, but unrecognized.

A talent may be there, but unrecognized.

FITTING INTO THE LEADERSHIP TEAM

It was emphasized earlier that leaders cannot operate effectively in isolation, certainly not at a working level. Yet research shows that more often than not leaders are appointed with scant consideration as to other members of the leadership team. Research also shows that, regardless of the caliber of the team leader, this can lead to disappointing, and sometimes disastrous, corporate leadership performance. No one is without fault or weakness, and unless those areas in which a leader is perhaps less strong are counterbalanced by another member of the leadership team, effectiveness suffers.

The leadership team, like any other team, depends for its effectiveness on the interaction of its component parts. The wise leader will appreciate this, and if in a position to do so will seek to balance the personalities and qualities in her or his leadership team, often seeking external advice in the process. Too often, though, leaders opt for the "comfort" factor and select like-minded and similar people to work with them.

Mix and Match

The following are a number of phrases used to describe successful leadership teams in the *Partners in Power* series of articles published in *The Times* in 1994.

"The team that mixes and matches ..."

"They work together in an easy rhythm. ... 'A' the realist, 'B' the dreamer etc. ... 'B' sketches ideas, ambitions ... 'A' talks about means, 'C' ..."

"It worked well because it was a blend of skills and chemistry."

"An unlikely combination ..."

"I am the one who is always pushing, and he is the one who holds back and asks questions."

"'A' came over as the hard-liner, 'B' as the adventurer."

THE DEVELOPMENT OF LEADERS

Just as it is important in our view that leaders should be assessed objectively for their potential, it is equally important for that potential to be developed in a positive and structured way, and not left to chance. The situation most often encountered sadly is the latter, reflecting perceptions and attitudes we have tried to argue against: that leadership is something you have (or lack) in some finite measure; or that experience in the job on its own is sufficient; or that development is a cost rather than an investment.

Perhaps it is worth considering the potential consequences of not consciously developing leaders (consequences that are valid at any level):

- Frustration both on the part of the individual and their subordinates which in turn can lead to unnecessary and unproductive stress.

- Underperformance by individual leaders, and pitching of their leadership and leadership thinking at a lower level than that required.

- Over-interference in the activities of subordinate leaders.

- An effect on both short and longer term corporate performance.

> *"The trouble is he doesn't know what his job is now that he has been promoted. He won't sit back and let us get on with our job. He's always interfering. Why can't he tell me what he wants, let me get on with it, and think a bit more about tomorrow and next week, where the real problems lie. I really can't work like this. No one knows who's in charge."*
>
> **A frustrated divisional manager**

Development guidelines

Leadership development, like any other development, should follow a number of guidelines:

- Organizations, even small ones, need a policy for recognizing the value of developing leaders, and a strategy on how that policy's aims should be met.

- Any person assuming higher level responsibilities will normally require appropriate development before or soon after assuming those responsibilities.

- Development should begin at the earliest point of need.

Development should begin at the earliest point of need.

- Development should be progressive, building on earlier development (where such has taken place), acknowledge experience, and reflect the changing needs at the next higher level.

- Development is a continuous process, not just a question of formal courses or seminars or training days. Most will therefore be on the job. This imposes a responsibility on the more senior who must accept the development of subordinates as a function of their appointment. Unfortunately, too few accept (or perhaps more accurately are aware of) that coaching role.

W H Smith is a UK company that has commendably for many years formally assessed its managers and at three levels:

- on entry;
- junior managers post experience;
- senior managers.

It has now moved onto a system that links performance appraisal, assessment and identification of individuals' development needs with individual development programs.

Formal development courses

Well-organized development training courses have considerable value at any level.

- They take the participants away from the distractions of the workplace and enable them to focus fully on the development program.

- Participants are able to think about issues and develop their own thoughts away from day-to-day pressures.

- Participants are able to benefit from peer group experience and discussion and the sharing of problems.

- They are usually conducted in an environment that is permissive of error.

- It is easier to involve the best tutors and facilitators.

The most effective courses are probably those organized and run in-company: they can be tailored specifically to an organization's requirements and its particular culture. Some companies and organizations are too small for this and have to resort to open courses at business schools, or with training and development organizations. The benefit here is the cross-fertilization that takes place between organizations. Whatever option is followed, there are a number of points that must be made:

- The course should be supervised by people with experience of the correct and appropriate level.

- If the course is being run in-company, the hierarchy of the organization should be directly involved.

- In the end, what is covered should be meaningful within the context of the workplace. This requires experienced tutoring and good facilitating of seminars and workshops (weak areas on many courses).

- The media of delivery used for development should not be allowed to become an end in themselves. This is a criticism that is made of many open courses, especially those using the outdoors as a medium, but also of other activities. The relevance of what is being done and what emerges must be clearly brought out.

Coaching

The coaching role of the leader was emphasized in an earlier chapter. Undoubtedly the key to successful leadership development is coaching, whether it be of a line manager by his divisional head, or of a new board member by the chairman. Yet as has been suggested already, it is a responsibility that is often neglected either through lack of thought or inclination. We all need guidance, no matter how senior, and especially when we are new or relatively new in the post. Most of us though can count on the fingers of one hand those who have acted in a positive way as coach or mentor in our own careers. All too often we are left to get on with the job, and have to determine best practice as best we can.

Obviously there are many styles of coaching that can be used depending on personalities and circumstances. The important thing is that it is done, and that it is done on a more or less continuous basis. If one were to assemble a group of middle or senior managers who are team leaders from a cross-section of organizations and enquire how often they receive what they might recognize as a on-the-job coaching, a positive response might come from perhaps one in five. That is the reality. Equally, only the same proportion will probably recognize their own coaching role to their subordinates! An excuse sometimes offered is that they fulfill that responsibility through the appraisal interview. That however is not enough, as it is likely to occur perhaps once a year. Meanwhile those being appraised work on as often as not unable to appreciate whether what they do is effective or otherwise, and being judged on that "untutored" performance.

An alternative means of coaching is growing slowly in popularity. Many senior people, particularly chairmen, executive and nonexecutive directors are discovering that skilled and completely confidential coaching by an individual outside the organization, can help to resolve leadership problems, including collective leadership. Internal coaching has often failed because of the sensitivities involved at the top of companies. A good consultant coach (and beware of charlatans) uses a mixed personal, philosophical and practical approach, based on his (the coach's) real experience. A good consultant generates confidence in the person coached to solve the problems themselves, as well as putting forward practical suggestions.

Performance check 6

RIGHT SELECTION AND DEVELOPMENT

1 When selecting others for positions of leadership, do you consciously balance objective evidence and subjective assessment?

2 How good is the appraisal system? Does it meet your organization's needs in assessing individuals' future leadership ability?

3 How far do you or your colleagues consciously seek individuals whose personality will complement the leadership abilities of others in the organization, rather than just bring the necessary technical competence?

4 Does your organization have a personnel development program, even at your level?

5 Do you encourage a coaching regime, formal or informal, in your area of responsibility? If not, should you?

Part IV

TRANSFORMING FOR THE MILLENNIUM

Good leadership will, if anything, become more necessary, and leading more difficult and certainly more demanding.

Chapter 12

◆

COLLECTIVE LEADERSHIP

OVERFOCUS ON THE INDIVIDUAL

We have so far concentrated on individual leaders and on the teams which leaders lead. There is a marked and understandable tendency to discuss and analyze leadership only in terms of the individual. Studies too generally focus on the person, on how effective A or B were or were not as leaders. There are, of course, many instances when this is rightly so. There are individuals who are given or acquire considerable personal authority or through circumstances or personality wield enormous personal influence and assume a dominant leadership role – not always with happy long-term results. And individuals, particularly dominant individuals, tend to excite far more interest than do groups. In reality, however, leadership is often more effectively practiced as a shared or group function, and not only in large organizations. It is that aspect of leadership which we now want to address.

DEFINING COLLECTIVE LEADERSHIP

Where there is collective leadership:

- power and responsibility are shared equally and collectively within the team;

- decisions are made and supported collectively;

- all members of a leadership team have a "generalist" function in addition to any specialist or representational role they may have;

- individual members of a leadership team must sublimate personal and functional interests to those of the group as a whole;

- there is a need for both individual and collective integrity, without which the team will lose its authority. If any member of the leadership team lacks integrity, the integrity of the whole team is weakened. The integrity of the collective leadership team is evident and exemplary in the way in which it exercises its function.

SHARING LEADERSHIP

In acknowledgment that different levels or dimensions of leadership require different talents or skills, or that some perform better in one leadership role than in another, or even that a particular leadership task is too large for one person, leadership is often shared between two or more individuals.

In the sporting field the playing captain, the team manager and the chairman all have their leadership roles within the overall leadership of a club. These roles are complementary, meeting different needs and requiring differing skills. They also operate within different time scales.

The same can be said of the boardroom where the chairman often has the responsibility for the strategic leadership of the organization, whereas the chief executive needs to focus more on the shorter term and exercise what might be described as operational leadership. There is a tendency, however, even in large companies, to avoid this sharing and allow an individual to fill both roles. This is in spite of the fact that it is still not overly common to find an individual who is able to meet the differing demands of the two roles effectively at the same time. This conclusion, amongst many others, was reinforced by the "Report of the Committee on *The Financial Aspects of Corporate Governance*" of 1992, and *Code of Best Practice*, known as the *Cadbury Code* – the authoritative document on running UK plcs, as required by the London Stock Exchange.

The Cadbury Code's recommendation of splitting the roles of chairman and chief executive is aimed not only at preventing one or the other from wielding too much power, but also at emphasizing the two different and distinctive roles.

"Chairmen should be able to stand sufficiently back from the day-to-day running of the business to ensure their boards are in full control of the company's affairs and alert to their obligations to their shareholders."[14]

It is difficult for a chairman/chief executive to stand back, and be wholly objective and independently minded. When things go wrong he is likely to be more protective of those who are responsible for the daily work of the company. He can also get into the habit of overlooking signs and warnings, which he thinks can be explained away if nonexecutives or shareholders happen to ask.

Barclay's Bank came under considerable pressure from its shareholders to split the role of Chairman and Chief Executive, which at the time was vested in a single person. The result was the establishment of a very effective leadership partnership to the benefit of both employees and shareholders.

It is surprising though how many large companies do not see the benefits of such a split. In smaller companies the need and perhaps the benefits are less obvious and of course it depends very much on size and type of business. Nevertheless, it is suggested that most companies and organizations above a "mean size" should adopt this recommendation. Even small companies have been seen to benefit from having someone, perhaps part-time and nonexecutive, catering for the strategic leadership needs.

It is often assumed that in companies run (and perhaps founded) by a strong or charismatic personality it is impossible to split the corporate leadership role. The reverse is often the case. Well-known figures such as Richard Branson and, latterly, Alan Sugar – the public "leadership face" of their companies – depend for their effectiveness on sharing their internal leadership role with others.

LEADERSHIP TEAMS

Another aspect of shared leadership is to be found in what we call the leadership team. Leadership at the top of institutions and organizations (including nations) is generally regarded as a group function. "The leadership" or "the management" is often used as a collective term in referring to a board, an executive committee, or even a Cabinet. This does not, of course, deny or negate the need for someone to be *primus inter pares*, the leader of the leadership team. But it does emphasize the sharing of leadership and its collective responsibility, and the interdependence of the members of the leadership teams for their overall effectiveness. Leadership teams, in other words, are like any other teams, as described earlier in Chapter 6.

> **Another aspect of shared leadership is to be found in what we call the leadership team.**

Whether the members of leadership teams always accept their

collective leadership role and responsibilities is another matter and the subject of considerable debate in recent years at both boardroom and national level. The former particularly appear to have suffered from a surfeit of overdominant personalities, and uncertainty, particularly over the teamplayer role of nonexecutive directors.

It could be argued that the later Cabinets of the Thatcher years suffered a loss of collective effectiveness because they ceased to operate fully as leadership teams.

> *"Every public company should be headed by an effective board which can both lead and control the business.*
>
> *The responsibilities of the board include – setting the company's strategic aims, providing the leadership that puts them into effect.*
>
> *Tests of board effectiveness include the way in which members of the board as a whole work together ... and their collective ability to provide ... the leadership ... which effective governance demands."*
>
> Report of the Committee on the Financial Aspects of
> Corporate Governance (The "Cadbury Report")[14]

A problem often encountered in top level leadership teams is persuading members of the group to sublimate the narrower interests of the departmental or other lower level teams for which individual members are responsible, to promote the broader needs of the organization. One of the main tasks of the team leader is to develop the necessary sense of corporate leadership responsibility, not always an easy undertaking.

> *"I cannot get my senior managers to act as a leadership team and think in terms of corporate leadership. Their only concern appears to be their own division and its*

171

> *future, not that of the Company. They will not act as*
> *a leadership team for the Company."*
> **Chairman of a medium-sized company (1993)**

It is a question of guiding, coaching and team building.

THE LEADERSHIP CENTER CONCEPT

While the concept and the need to share leadership and operate as leadership teams are becoming accepted fairly widely at the top of organizations, the same cannot be said lower down the structures where the focus of leadership tends to be still very much on the individual. We believe there is a strong need to change this culture, recognized already in some of the better run companies.

Essentially we see an extension of the idea of Financial Responsibility Centers already introduced into many companies (namely investment, budget, project, cost, revenue, and profit centers) into the field of leadership, with an acceptance of Leadership Centers or teams at each level of management. This takes effective teamworking a stage further.

The purpose of a Leadership Center is to improve the quality of organizational leadership at each and every level of management. Each Center would involve in the leadership process, the leader or leader representatives of those agencies whose interests should have a direct influence on, or are directly affected by operational decision-making at that level. These are often people who might not normally see themselves as having a leadership role or being part of a leadership team.

The purpose of a Leadership Center is to improve the quality of organizational leadership at each and every level of management.

172

Centers would not operate in isolation: they would be part of an integrated network of Centers. Each Center leader would normally be a member of a Center at the next higher level. Each Center member would be leader of a lower level Center or participate as a member in other teams, or perhaps both. There is liaison between Centers, for example, in sharing best practice.

The objectives of the Leadership Centers are:

- to improve the quality of advice given to higher level Centers as part of the input to decision-making at the higher level;
- to enable decisions at their own level to be based on best advice through active participation of all interested and affected parties;
- to share collective responsibility for any decisions made;
- to lay down parameters and objectives (but not methodology) for the next lower level Center or work unit;
- to evaluate performance against objectives.

This does not in any way conflict with the idea of self-managed teams, indeed it greatly complements it: the Centers are giving direction, not detailing how a task should be done. The direction, however, is the same direction throughout the whole company or organization.

The outcome, we believe, would be a greatly increased realization of the energy inherent in any organization. The "currency" here is leadership. In diagrammatic form the structure in an organization could be as shown overleaf.

The 'currency' here is leadership.

Some organizations have moved in this direction: UNIPART has set up a large number of designated Stakeholder Circles. The focus in these groups is very much on team rather than individual or leader responsibility, and the teams themselves share problem-solving and are sufficiently empowered to make operational decisions – which is what "empowerment" should be about. The Stakeholder Circles go far beyond the Quality Circles that have enjoyed a degree of fashion.

The Structure of Leadership Centers

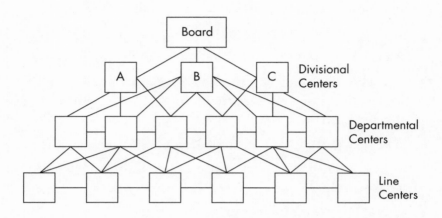

Solid lines indicate Leadership/Communication flow. While shown as single dimensional in this diagram, the Leadership Centers will be multi-dimensional and lines drawn connecting all or most Leadership Centers.

At the other end of the spectrum is a company that we visited recently. Here the middle management team allocated no time to discussion prior to decision-making, explaining decisions or reviewing completed projects. Each member focussed narrowly on his or her own task, the team leader was inaccessible and, as a result, the team generally was underperforming.

But the idea of Leadership Centers as part of the corporate structure cannot just happen. It requires education and training of leaders and managers, particularly those in the middle and lower ranks who tend to feel most pressurized and who might feel threatened by what they perceive to be an undermining of their authority. Removing some of the (unnecessary) layers of management also helps! It also requires a corporate environment that is open, has excellent communication systems, and is permissive of failure to the extent that error is used as a vehicle for learning and improvement. The essence therefore of Leadership Centers is participation and collective responsibility.

Given the nature of their work, particularly on the operational side, responsibility for leadership in the uniformed services is perhaps inevitably vested in individuals. We would suggest nevertheless that in nonoperational circumstances – the majority of the time – and even in some operational situations the concept of Leadership Centers could and should be applied.

SUPPORTING LEADERSHIP TEAMS

What the Armed Services in particular have been good at is in developing an extremely effective leadership support organization, their so-called staff system. Staff officers are selected and trained more for their support than leadership skills *per se* (although many are effective leaders) and provide advice to their commanders that is well researched and independent of departmental interests. If properly selected, they complement the personality of their leader, and are in effect an extension of the personality of the leader. They also enable the leader to focus more on key issues. It is arguably an overlavish system from a nonmilitary point of view and is designed to cope with rather different circumstances – including the "just in case" aspect of extreme military contingencies rather than the "just-in-time" concept of reducing costs. Nevertheless, it is a system from which the nonuniformed sectors could learn, especially larger organizations.

The staff system

"The staff officer assists his commander (i.e. chief executive) by:

a. Understanding his commander's future requirements and offering informed advice when called for, or if an important factor has been overlooked.

b. Providing the commander with information to assist him in reaching decisions, whilst making his own decisions within his delegated areas of responsibility, thus protecting the commander from irrelevant detail.

c. Developing and implementing the commander's plan by issuing and monitoring the execution of directives and orders on his behalf.

The staff must be the servants of the troops, and that a good staff officer must serve his commander and the troops but must himself be anonymous."

Command – **A UK Army Doctrine Publication**

Performance check 7

COLLECTIVE LEADERSHIP

1 How effective are you and the organization at sharing the leadership function? Is the concept of leadership teams accepted?

2 Do all members of leadership teams
- understand their role
- accept the responsibilities involved and
- subordinate their other interests to those of the team?

3 Do the leadership teams really work as an entity? Are there divisions, and if so can you identify their cause?

4 Are the leadership teams properly supported in staff terms?

5 Can you identify existing (but undesignated) Leadership Centers in your organization? How easily could they be built into the existing structure? Would the concept capture the imagination of your colleagues and be made to work effectively?

Chapter 13

◆

BOARDROOM LEADERSHIP

"Every public company should be headed by a board which can both lead and control the business."

The Cadbury Report[14]

AT THE TOP

A number of times in this book we have referred to the leadership role of directors, mainly in the context of strategic leadership. In this chapter we want to focus specifically on those in this group, be they in the public or private sector, in commercial or noncommercial organizations, in small companies or large. We do so in view of the doubts so often raised about how far one can use the term "leadership" in the boardroom and as a contribution to current debate. Some of the points we make are a repetition of ones made earlier in a more general context, but they are included again here for completeness. Others are more specific to the boardroom.

Directors do of course come in many guises and number many tens of thousands. They range from executive directors who are main board members in large multinational companies, to nonexecutive directors of public sector trusts and charities, to sole directors of small family businesses. Regardless of the size

179

of the organization or the nature of the directorship they all have functional similarities recognized in law.

THE DIRECTOR'S ROLE

Directors have more of a leadership than a management function. Indeed, directors as such are not managers *per se*. The directors' representative body in the UK, the Institute of Directors, talks generally of the leadership responsibilities of directors in creating wealth for the benefit of business and society as a whole. We suggest that all boards of directors, regardless of the nature or size of the organization, have a number of specific leadership functions. These include:

> **Directors have more of a leadership than a management function.**

- the creation of the vision for the organization; what does it want to be?
- establishing objectives;
- determining the strategy and developing policies to meet the objectives and fulfill the vision;
- setting standards;
- guiding and monitoring the way in which the organization operates;
- major decision-making;
- selecting those for key operational leadership positions.

This implies taking a long-term strategic view, and a relative detachment from immediate operations, which should be the clear responsibility of management. Unfortunately, however, in many organizations the focus is at best mid- rather than long-term, and in business this often means preoccupations with short-term profitability, frequently in response to pressure from the financial markets. Creation of a vision and investment in the people, resources and research which are so essential to meet long-term goals, take lower priorities.

> *"Too many plc boards use meetings to discuss operational items. This means that long term ... strategic issues are not given sufficient emphasis.*

A director

We have noticed an increasing acknowledgment of the seriousness of directors' responsibilities since the publication in 1992 of the Cadbury Committee's *Report on the Financial Aspects of Corporate Governance*. While some aspects were unpopular – directors do not like being preached at – there is a recognition that best practice includes both probity as well as profit.

THE BOARD

In Chapter 12 we suggested that the board of directors represents an excellent model of a leadership team. The board exemplifies collective leadership, shared decision-making and collective responsibility. That is the theory – and the practice in better organizations. Sadly though, it is probably not the norm, although all directors on any given board have a shared legal responsibility for its workings and actions. The board is a collective legal entity.

> **The board exemplifies collective leadership, shared decision-making and collective responsibility. That is the theory – and the practice in better organizations.**

Some boards

"I have found that there is often a not very effective mix of talent on boards, particularly in small companies."

"More often than not politics rule the board."

"Introspection normally only takes place when a situation is near crisis."

"Powerful people often don't like their view of an issue challenged, or even debated."

"I was invited to be a non-executive director of a plc, and ended up as chairman and chief executive, having to fire the rest of the board."

Authors' interviews with board directors

From a nine-nation study it was discovered that far from being actually dishonest and secretive

"more than half British directors ... said problems damaging to the business were never raised, because it would be too difficult ... they are emotionally unable to do so."

Prof Kakabadse, Cranfield School of Management

A fundamental point we would wish to make is that those accepting appointments as board directors should both understand and accept their role as part of the collective leadership team of the organization and the individual and collective responsibility that goes with it. We feel many do not.

We quoted earlier the comment of one chairman who could not get the executive members of his board to sublimate their divisional interests to those of the company as a whole. This, sadly, is not an uncommon experience. To an extent it may be a failure of training or briefing. Some agencies recommend that anyone becoming a director has to be given written guidance as to their role and responsibilities, and sign to that effect.

NON-EXECUTIVE DIRECTORS

The problem is perhaps greatest among non-executive directors who either do not see themselves as part of the leadership team or, more probably, are not accepted as such by the executive directors. Their independence can be resented. Their role is certainly misunderstood. But, perhaps more importantly, it is the executive directors who often do not understand the strategic leadership role of the board, their main preoccupation being with direct operational leadership and management.

"I do not regard the non-executive directors as part of the leadership team. That is the job of the executive directors."

Chief Executive of a large plc

Admittedly, some non-executive directors are only there for the perks and easy remuneration. This number is dwindling fast, particularly after the publication of the Report of the Cadbury Committee. We argue that a majority want to play a more active leadership role. This is borne out by some major research we have undertaken – *Coming on Board: The Non-Executive Directors' Role in Strengthening Boardroom Leadership* (1995). Even family nonexecutives in the smaller companies are having to work hard nowadays.

"For an NED to bring out real, hard thinking (amongst the board) requires him to be persistent, to have done his homework thoroughly, and to be properly supported by the chairman."

An experienced non-executive director

183

One non-executive director stated that "a non-executive director is only as good as the information he or she holds." But how many are given sufficient information? It is often in the perceived short-term interests of an executive director to steamroller matters through a board. And what better way to do so than by depriving the non-executive directors and executive colleagues of important information that might undermine the case when viewed strategically?

> It is often in the perceived short-term interests of an executive director to steamroller matters through a board.

We acknowledge readily that there is a growing awareness of the non-executive directors' role and value especially in the larger companies. But their value, is still underappreciated generally, particularly in smaller organizations. As far as the larger organizations are concerned, there have been a number of well-publicized cases in recent years where non-executive directors have displayed their real worth, and incidentally the authority they can acquire and leadership they can exercise. BP is one such case which comes to mind.

A danger inherent in any unitary board system is that the leadership team becomes split between executive and non-executive elements. It ceases then to be an effective team. Arguably, the same is likely to happen if the boardroom team is too large. We noted in an earlier chapter that this was a feature of too large teams. A welcome trend seems to be a move towards smaller boards, possibly in acknowledgment of this characteristic.

THE LEADER OF THE BOARD

The key person on the board is – or should be – the chairman. It is he or she who is the leader of the leadership team, with all that this implies. The chairman is the person who should be instru-

mental in developing the effectiveness of the team, even if he or
she lacks executive authority – as
many do. It is the chairman who
should ensure that the real leader-

**The key person on the
board is – or should be –
the chairman.**

ship role of the board is kept in view, who guides the discussion,
who encourages openness, who should avoid partiality, and
who should ensure that the board faces up to rather than avoids
the real issues. And, importantly, when the roles are split, the
chairman should avoid becoming just the mouthpiece of the
chief executive. But are chairmen appointed always with these
points in mind?

One of the most difficult problems faced by any board is how
to work effectively with a strong, dominant personality, whether
it be the chairman or chief execu-
tive. In commercial life particularly the chances are that anyone
who is at the top has a certain
strength of will – otherwise they
would not be where they are. This
does not deny, of course, that
there may be other reasons for
their being there. Unfortunately,
this can have damaging consequences as we have seen in some
recent and highly publicized
court cases. But no matter how

**One of the most difficult
problems faced by any
board is how to work
effectively with a strong,
dominant personality,
whether it be the
chairman or chief
executive.**

strong or dominant the personality, this does not absolve the
other directors from their legal leadership responsibilities. This,
of course, is where the nonexecutive directors – whose future is
usually less dependent on the dominant personality – can play
their part by exercising moral courage, but then that is expected
of leaders anyway. They should exert their independence if necessary by resigning. The problem may be compounded by the
composition of the board. A tendency among dominant (as

opposed to strong) personalities is to surround themselves with sycophants or certainly with likeminded people. This raises the question of selection: how does the board ensure that it has a balanced team, in terms of both experience and personality? Is selection self-perpetuating, or an objectively conducted exercise? These are questions to which many boards have still not found the answers. We refer back to the discussion on team composition and selection in Chapter 6.

> **A tendency among dominant (as opposed to strong) personalities is to surround themselves with sycophants or certainly with likeminded people.**

In larger organizations the boardroom is at the pinnacle of a network of leadership teams. As such it sets the leadership tone of an organization in terms of style and ethos. It also provides the basis of its ethical stand by its policies and example. Sadly, the latter has been visibly weak in some organizations, not least in the areas of remuneration and financial probity.

TEAMBUILDING

No matter how experienced are the individual members of the board, in most cases there is still need to develop them as a team for it to be fully effective. Boards are like any other teams. There is a need too for individual directors to participate in personal training programs to enable them to play their part fully. This is especially important when first appointed as director – it can be a very big step for someone whose experience has been limited to line or functional management. Our major research project found that 83 per cent of directors questioned acknowledged that specific director training is required when first joining a board. Updating every two or three years and special non-executive training was recommended by more than 60 per cent. This presents another task for the chairman, the team leader to arrange.

> "I was delighted to be appointed to the main board but for some months I didn't really know what my role was. As a result I kept my mouth shut and didn't contribute much. It was only after about 18 months that I found my feet and gained the confidence to really participate in board meetings."
>
> Executive director of a large plc

Performance check 8

ON BOARD

1 Is the board totally fulfilling its leadership role? Is it addressing the long term, determining strategic aims and developing appropriate policies, and setting appropriate goals?

2 Is the board functioning as a leadership team? Does it see itself as such? Would it benefit from team building?

3 Where there are non-executive members of the board, are they truly accepted as part of the collective leadership, and do they in turn accept the role and responsibilities?

4 Are new members of the board adequately briefed and coached as to their role?

5 Have you considered training for board members? If not, why not?

Chapter 14

◆

LEADERSHIP 2000

A PARADOX?

It is tempting to assume that leading will become easier and leadership less necessary in a world and in societies that are increasingly well educated and sophisticated, with global and instant communication, widespread access to information, and growing international awareness. In fact, the opposite is probably true. How will traditional leadership ideas fare in societies in which many will demand and be offered greater control over their own lives and jobs? How can leaders allow increasing scope for the individual efforts of others?

> It is tempting to assume that leading will become easier and leadership less necessary.

Good leadership will, if anything, become more necessary, and leading more difficult and certainly more demanding. Why this apparent contradiction? These very same sociological, cultural and technological developments, widely welcome and beneficial though they may be, can serve equally to increase feelings of doubt or undermine certainty and confidence in people's minds. Such is the price of progress and change and the need for leadership. The developments and changes may be of a gradual rather than dramatic nature but their effect will nevertheless be considerable even over a relatively short time span.

THE WORLD OF WORK

A considerable amount has been written already about tomorrow's workplace and the world of work in the future. "The thinking company," "the learning company," "an information-based society" are the sort of terms with which we are becoming increasingly familiar. Indeed, some companies and organizations are already adopting approaches and introducing systems that are a radical departure from the past, usually as part of promoting "best practice" and reflecting both changing social conditions, and the effects of technological development. But what effect will this have on leadership?

Let us look first at some of the changes we are likely to see. The workforce is likely to become demonstrably better educated and trained generally although for some years to come there will be a sizeable albeit gradually decreasing pool of those who are under-educated and untrained. To some this might appear to be an idealized projection, but the policies already set in train in many countries, the pressures for further improvements and widespread political support make this a reasonable assumption.

Better education is accompanied normally by a desire for more information and an increased facility to absorb it. That desire is heightened as we become an information-based society.

One of the pressures for change in the UK is the transformation of the jobs market, and we have witnessed already a considerable decline in the numbers employed in manufacturing (but not necessarily in manufacturing capacity) and a steady growth in the numbers employed in the professional and service sectors. Even in the service sector there has been a degree of realignment, and ironically we could well see a growth in some areas of jobs that demand few or less skill levels (such as domestic support), although in the main growth has been and will be in those areas demanding greater knowledge and skills.

Whatever the work, manpower is likely to be less intensively distributed due primarily to the introduction of new technologies and associated restructuring that has been going on and is set to continue. The pattern of work will also change further: an increase in outsourcing, of home working, in job sharing, and in people having more than one job.

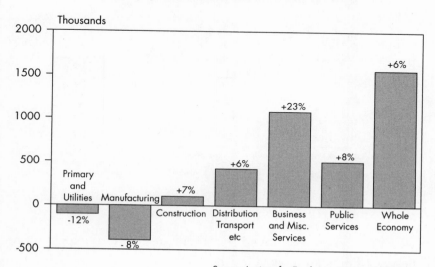

Overall Employment Change 1993–2001 (UK)

Source: Institute for Employment Research 1994

Jobs for life are already almost a thing of the past, and most people will have two or three careers, with a larger proportion than hitherto working on a self-employed or short-contract basis. Those who do stay on in companies are more likely to have to accept moves sideways and downwards rather than necessarily upwards. The demand for

Jobs for life are already almost a thing of the past.

early retirement from work generally (rather than from a particular form of employment) on the other hand might well decrease, as the pressures of a relatively smaller workforce and an aging population increase.

Change in Employment by Occupation 1993–2001 (UK)

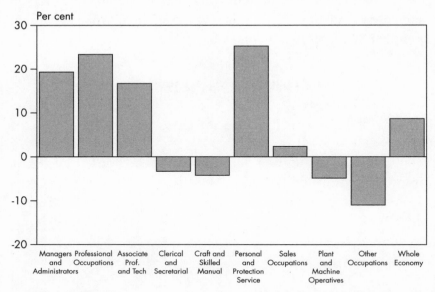

Note: Excludes Armed Forces   Source: Institute for Employment Research 1994

Those who are employed by others are likely to expect more than just financial reward for their labours:

- a better "package" including company-provided welfare;
- a greater say in the running of the organization;
- an emphasis on good working conditions.

This is likely to be accompanied by improved employee protection. Actual financial rewards will be increasingly based in part on performance, and an equable share of profit. Ironically, perhaps, there could well be a placing of greater value on contribution rather than merely assessable skills, with the pattern of reward reflecting this. Thus the

Thus the dustman, postman, milkman and the cleaning lady will enjoy a better status than they do perhaps today – a trend we are seeing already.

192

dustman, postman, milkman and the cleaning lady will enjoy a better status than they do perhaps today – a trend we are seeing already.

CULTURAL BLENDING

One of the more noticeable social features in the past few years has been a gradual coming together of national cultures, especially among young people. This has been brought about by improved education and communications, the effect of which is likely to grow and spread. Nevertheless, it may take another generation, and longer in some closed or controlled societies, for the impact on behavior and attitudes generally to become really significant. It is likely to have a more immediate impact, however, on the commercial and business world, and we may within a very few years be in a position to describe a company as truly international. We are likely to witness, too, the growth of the truly international business school, and multinational degree and other courses in universities and colleges. At the same time, we may see a lessening of some of the artificialities (often expensive artificialities) and other aspects associated with international working and introduced as a means of overcoming cultural barriers. Other cultural and subcultural phenomena, however, will spring up, together with new artificialities.

LEADERSHIP DEMANDS

So what does this mean? We emphasized in Chapter 4 the varying nature of the environment in which leadership is practiced and the need for leaders to be able to react or adapt to the changes in that environment. In that sense nothing is altered. We also emphasized the need for leaders to be able to lead others through periods of change. Again, the same principle still applies, But the extent of the challenge might be greater.

We are seeing already an increased willingness to define leadership needs and to question the leader's performance. This affects all walks of life, and headlines such as "Wanted – Leadership," "The Lost Leader," and "M fails the Leadership Test" are becoming increasingly common. Leaders are being called to account more, and being made more accountable.

In the commercial and business fields the PR exercise that passed for an annual general meeting in many public companies appears to be on its way out. Chairmen and chief executives are being made to justify their leadership and leadership decisions. There is a trend too towards making leaders and leadership teams legally as well as morally liable for their decisions and actions. Leadership responsibility is being written into codes of corporate behavior. Cosy, unquestioned leadership is unlikely to feature much. Even those in the professions are unlikely to be spared.

We have observed already change in three particular aspects of leadership:

- openness;
- persuasion;
- sharing.

By openness we mean greater sharing of information, deeper consultation before decision making on key issues and indeed on any issues affecting the lives of others, and explanation of decisions arrived at. Good communication will be at a premium, and it will need to become a continuous process. The "stakeholder" concept, little understood in the UK, will grow in importance, since it incorporates much of the above criteria.

Because people in the main will have greater freedom of choice and more control or ownership of their own lives they will have to be persuaded rather than coerced, although obviously some scope for coercion will always exist. Loyalty to an organization or team will be the outcome of that persuasion and will frequently need to be renewed. Moral leadership will be expected, with integrity and example high on the list. The emphasis will be on the responsibilities of leadership, not on privilege or perks. Codes of ethics will be the norm, and enforced rather than just having lip service paid to them.

Moral leadership will be expected, with integrity and example high on the list.

We are seeing already a greater emphasis on sharing which is linked closely to openness and persuasion, but goes further. The emphasis will be on sharing not only information and decision-making but also leadership itself: an emphasis on leadership teams, delegation, and teamworking.

We are seeing already a greater emphasis on sharing which is linked closely to openness and persuasion, but goes further.

"We make people feel that they do matter, and not just inside the company. We like to ensure all stakeholders have the same objectives. The five key relationships are with our stakeholders, the shareholders, staff, suppliers, customers and the community. We are all working for sustainable success. We have set up 'stakeholder circles' [mirroring quality circles] to ensure things go well." A subsidiary Premier Exhausts of Birmingham which performed extremely badly in 1989 improved to be one of the best producers in 1994.

Royal Society of Arts, *Tomorrow's Company*[13]

TEAMLEADING AND TEAMWORKING

Although we are seeing already a welcome re-emergence of the team and with it an emphasis on teamworking as a concept, leadership of teams will not necessarily be made any easier. If anything, and as we suggested earlier, it will become more demanding. We have mentioned the challenge of developing team loyalty in the changed society we foresee. The challenge will be the greater in those organizations in which teams, and often individual team members, are widely dispersed and perhaps more inwardly focussed through the increased use of advanced technology and changed work practices.

Multiteam membership and a growing awareness of interteam dependence increase the challenge. Perhaps the greatest demand therefore will be for leadership development and team building. No longer will these be in the "nice to do but we cannot afford the time – or the money" category. Rather, they will be seen as essential activities in any organization that wishes to succeed.

Tomorrow's Leader

- "Can you mediate emotional issues without taking sides or picking favorites?

- Can you breathe freely and remain relaxed even in the presence of passionate fears and desires?

- Are your own conflicts clarified? Is your own house clean?

- Can you be gentle with all factions and lead the group without dominating?

- Can you remain open and receptive, no matter what issues arise?

- Can you know what is emerging, yet keep your peace while others discover for themselves?

- Learn to lead in a nourishing manner.

- Learn to lead without being possessive.

- Learn to be helpful without taking the credit.

- Learn to lead without coercion.

You can do this if you remain unbiased, clear, and down-to-earth."

Lao Tzu, 5th century BC

Plus ça change.

Chapter 15

◆

MEASURING UP

TAKING STOCK

In writing this book we set out to stimulate thinking on what we regard as a vitally important area of human activity and, even more importantly, to help executives and others in a wide variety of fields to improve their individual and collective leadership performance. Some of you will, of course, be effective leaders already, others consciously less so. Of the former, even the best are likely to have some shortcomings, and our experience of those in this category has been that they are usually the most anxious to evaluate and improve their performance.

Whatever your performance level, an important exercise that any individual or group in a position of leadership should carry out on a regular basis is to pose themselves a number of questions, and to validate their responses through people who are likely to give honest rather than sycophantic answers – it is so easy to delude oneself or be persuaded that there are no problems, especially if you are in the top position!

> **It is so easy to delude oneself or to be persuaded that there are no problems, especially if you are in the top position!**

Such an exercise obviously requires a degree of confidence but also of humbleness on the part of individuals, but these are qualities displayed anyway by effective leaders.

APPROPRIATE QUESTIONS

The sort of questions we should be asking ourselves are:

1 Do I, or we as a leadership team, know where we want to be in five, ten, fifteen years time? Do we have a clear vision of our future as an organization? Is that vision being communicated adequately to the rest of the organization?

2 Have we determined a clear set of goals or objectives that we need to meet to enable us to fulfill that vision?

3 Do we have a clear direction as to how we are going to get where we want to be and is this accepted and understood by all? Or have we lost sight of our objectives?

4 Is everyone working in the same direction? Is our communication effective? Is it regularly programmed in? Are we getting through to all levels?

5 Have I had any meaningful discussion of late with people at least two levels down?

6 Does everyone seem part of the team (team in the widest sense)?

7 Is the team working as a cohesive unit? Is anyone or group not pulling their weight? If so, have I tried to find out why? Is the team at all stale? Does it require a team-building boost?

8 Have we been avoiding making any key decisions?

9 Of those decisions that have been made, was there adequate consultation beforehand and explanation subsequently? Did everyone who should participate in the decision-making? Was the groundwork for decision-making well done?

10 Have I allowed sufficient unprogrammed time in my diary?

11　Have I been out and about enough? Or has my diary been driving me?

12　Have I been sufficiently accessible? Has everyone who wanted to been able to see me? Has my office been over-protecting me?

13　Have I visited my subordinates in their own offices / premises?

14　Have I spent any time discussing performance with / coaching those for whom I am directly responsible?

15　Are there any areas in which I could have delegated more? In those areas in which I have exercised delegation, have I kept a watching brief? Or have I interfered too much?

16　Have we assessed thoroughly recent work and absorbed lessons learnt?

17　Have I given adequate recognition for achievement or expressed sufficient gratitude for outstanding effort or application?

18　Are there any aspects of the organization's operation or performance with which I am unhappy? If so, have I done anything about it?

This list is by no means exhaustive; there are no doubt other questions you would wish to add. The important point is that you should go through such an exercise, and on a regular basis. No one is too senior or cannot benefit, not even national leaders!

Only you will know the answers. And as we quoted at the beginning of this book, "There is nobody who cannot vastly improve his powers of leadership by a little thought and practice."

> **No one is too senior or cannot benefit, not even national leaders!**

"The task of leadership is not to put greatness into humanity, but to elicit it, for the greatness is already there."

John Buchan

and finally:

"The final test of a great leader is that he leaves behind him in other men the will to carry on."

Walter Lippman writing on Franklin D. Roosevelt

APPENDIX

◆

LEADERSHIP RESEARCH

Why research?

We deliberately avoided an academic style in this book, while quietly having at the back of our minds the fact that behavioral research helps to validate the intuitional and pragmatic practice of leadership, and assists in our understanding of how effective leaders lead.

Behavior

Serious research on leadership was initially a by-product of work study, conducted in the US in the late 1920s, of the behavior of people in their daily work routines in large organizations. The studies by Elton Mayo and others in the Western Electric Plant at Hawthorne, Ohio discovered significant facts about the norms and variables of work.

In the post-war years the University of Michigan conducted a research program over a period of twenty years, with results quantified by behavioral statistical scales. Rensis Likert summarized the studies by dividing leading groups into **Task-orientated behavior, Relationship-orientated behavior** and **Participative Leadership**. The Ohio State University program started later and concentrated on the refinement of the questionnaire as a tool to measure **attitudes on behavior and leadership,** thus bringing to the public's notice that – in the field of leadership as in any field – **attitudes** do not necessarily reflect **actual behavior** and vice-versa. In Britain war leaders and a few academics were promoting a more pragmatic approach, basing their generalizations on a mixture of acute observation and insight, prioritizing the traits of named leaders.

Traits, skills and motivation research

This approach to leadership study, depending on who was conducting it, instinctively deliberately followed studies in motivation: Abraham Maslow, with his hierarchy of needs from the "physiological" to the "self-actualization" (or self-fulfillment); Douglas McGregor, with his **x and y theories** of external motivation by coercion/control/money against self-motivation and a deeply understanding regime; Frederick Herzberg with his research which concluded with his division of **motivation factors** and **hygiene factors**, (the latter being the circumstances under which people worked, i.e. good conditions or bad).

The trait approach involves extensive debate about adjectives and nouns describing what a leader is or possesses (integrity, loyalty, capacity for hard work etc). The link with motivational research was the individual leader's personal disposition towards motivating his (in those days very much "his") team. R. L. Katz and F. C. Mann differentiated the **interpersonal skills** from the knowledge and understanding of people and their use of **technical skills** (techniques and processes) and **conceptual skills** (analytical, creativity, handling of ambiguity). The value of synthesizing the trait, skills and motivation research with behavioral analysis in further work study is self-evidently helpful. So much for the leaders, what about the followers?

Power-influence

In previous generations, power and leadership were strongly

linked. As social **status** gave way to a more **contractual** basis for society, (noted by Sir Henry Maine in the nineteenth century) and the experience of two world wars shook thinking people into questioning how much power individual leaders should possess, so a more functional and objective approach was developed. Power was defined by researchers like John Kotter and Henry Mintzberg, and **positional power** was differentiated from **personal power**. But dividing personality too far from the individual's position was unsatisfactory. J. R. P. French and H. H. Raven cataloged categories of power – i.e. reward, coercive, legitimate, expert and referent – the latter being the emotional-identity link between leader and led. J. K. Galbraith, on a different plane, differentiated between "condign (punishment)/compensatory power and conditional power," noting that the sources are "personality, property and organization." The complexities of the **influence** of the leader over the led has been a perennial line for researchers, and this brings us on to the "situational approach."

Situational

This line of research deduces that a leader is faced with particular circumstances depending on the nature of the work itself, the actual environment (including level of risk) and the characteristics of the real and individual people in the team – **dependent or independent variables**. A strong theme has been linking **human agency and contingency theories**, the preserve hitherto of philosophers. M. G. Evans, R. J. House and T. R. Mitchell in the 1970s devised and extended from their research the **path-goal theory**, which, taking account of the situational/personal variables, led to four types of leadership, viz **supportive, directive, participative** and **achievement-orientated leadership**.

The other major theory to be codified from research is by Frederick Fiedler. He devised and rested exhaustively the **LPC Model**, the "least-preferred co-worker" or "colleague," which in any group shows up pecking-orders and a popularity scale between individuals. Based on a scale, the sum of individual scores showed not only individual popularity (for whatever reason, including competence in the job), but how closely or divergently the team worked: too great a difference in scores shows a team that is not well integrated. Based on the knowledge of the leader about individuals, the leader then **takes effective action** to improve the team's cohesiveness and effectiveness.

This is in line with the **Action Centered Leadership** model of Professor John Adair, devised at the Royal Military Academy Sandhurst from the 1960s. It is based on the dependent variables of the **task, team** and **individual's needs**. The action the leader takes to satisfy individual needs diminishes the divisiveness which would otherwise infect the team, in divergent personal agendas and weaknesses. This is as applicable at boardroom level as it is for small groups working on practical projects. The contribution to the situational approach to leadership theory is the research by P. Hersey and K. H. Blanchard in the 1980s on degrees of **maturity of individuals**, that is how able and willing are team members to share **high degrees of responsibility** with the leader. This links the McGregor x and y theory, that more people than was hitherto expected are or can be very responsible towards their role, job and organization. It also links with the maturity of the group, i.e. how long and well the procedures are established and kept updated. All of these factors are significant in our experience of **collective leadership** and the **Leadership Center** concept and practice.

Participative leadership

All the above leads on to the research conducted to validate the **participative leadership** style achieved or attempted by many organizations, particularly in recent years. The notable collaborative researchers in this field are F. Heller and G. A. Yukl, and V. H. Vroom and P. W. Yetton. The findings are on a sliding scale of

decision-making practice. At one end is the **autocratic decision;** it moves through **consultation,** and **joint-decision** to **delegation**. We believe that not enough research has gone into the art of delegation and the new instinctively differentiated **empowerment**. Is this latter more psychological than substantial?

Charismatic leadership

Derived from the belief in the trait theories, this is to do with the unique inspirational and public personality of leaders who get things done quickly. While difficult to differentiate from autocratic power, R. N. Kanungo and J. A. Conger have been the leading researchers in this field. The latter concluded that the traits and behaviors are "interpersonal relationships, impulsive and unconventional behavior, high self-confidence and impressive performance." There are both **positive aspects** and **negative consequences** of charismatic leadership. Such leaders also tend to be egocentric to a fault and short on attention to detail; succession planning, if considered at all, can fail.

Transformational leadership

The researchers Burns and Bass noted that the **transaction** of rewards for compliance between leader and led was too much to do with power and not enough about influence. Burns concluded that in **transformational** leadership, "leaders and followers raise **one another** to higher levels of **morality and motivatation**." This raises the subject of **agency theory,** that all people are in some way **moral agents**. The change of a culture of transactional leadership to one of **transformational leadership culture**, is largely the work and findings of Schein in recent years. The ethical culture or **ethos** of an organization, as distinct from **kratos**, the real world of behavior and practice falling far short of the ideal, leads one to the current thinking about **corporate governance** and the responsibilities at the highest level of organizations. Their role is to create wealth and subscribe to the highest values. The organization's **vision and mission** are set by the designated leaders, individually or collectively. If realized, it follows that the leadership throughout the organization is fully effective.

NOTES AND REFERENCES

◆

1 See Charles Hampden Turner, *Charting the Corporate Mind*, Blackwell, Oxford, 1990, p. 155.

2 J. P. Kotter, *The General Managers*, Free Press/Macmillan, New York, 1982, p. 35. This title and the book referenced in Note 1 are seminal works about generalist/specialist skills and generalists/specialists.

3 Dr G. G. Kullmann, "The Challenge of Leadership in our Time," *Walker Trust Lectures on Leadership*, No, III, 1931. This excellent series was delivered annually at the University of St Andrews in the 1930s and 1940s.

4 In David A. Whetton and Kim S. Cameron, *Developing Management Skills*, Harper Collins, New York, 1991.

5 J. P. Kotter "What Leaders Really Do," *Harvard Business Review*, May/June, 1990.

6 Larue Tone Hosmer, *The Ethics of Management*, Irwin, Boston MA, 1991, p. 103.

7 Alan L. Frohman and Leonard W. Johnson, *The Middle Management Challenge: Moving from Crisis to Empowerment*, McGraw Hill, New York, 1993, p. 110.

8 "Personality intensive" is an organizational description which one of our authors discovered in research and a clinical trial in 1983 for the Armed Forces. Independently, Richard Normann, author of *Service Management: Strategy and Leadership in Service Business*, Chichester/New York, John Wiley, 1984, has also defined it. The description is of a different category order to the more usual "capital intensive/labor intensive" descriptors of organizations.

9 See F. Herzberg's *The Motivation to Work*, Wiley, New York, 1959.

10 John R. Katzenbach and Douglas K. Smith, *The Wisdom of Teams: Creating the High Performance Organisation*, Harvard Business School Press, Boston MA, 1993, p. 3.

11 See Dorwin Cartwright and Alvin Zander (eds), *Group Dynamics: Research and Theory*, New York, Harper and Row / Harper Collins, 1953. W. J. Sprott's *Human Groups*, London, Pelican, 1958–77, is also a useful book.

12 See Richard Normann, *Service Management* (1984), op. cit. The author's theme is shown analogously as a matador facing the bull – he is facing reality, here and now.

13 From "Shared Destinies," *Tomorrow's Company*, London, Royal Society of Arts, 1995.

14 *Report of the Committee on the Financial Aspects of Corporate Governance, The Cadbury Committee*, London, Gee, December 1992, p. 21.

FURTHER READING

◆

Adair, John, *Not Bosses but Leaders*, Guildford, Talbot Adair Press, 1987.

Adair, John, *Action Centred Leader*, London, Pan, 1983.

Adair, John, *Great Leaders*, Guildford, Talbot Adair Press, 1989.

Badarocco, Joseph L., Jnr and Ellsworth, Richard R., *Leadership and the Quest for Integrity*, Boston, Harvard Business School, 1989.

Belbin, Meredith, *Management Teams: Why They Succeed or Fail*, London, Heinemann, 1981.

Bennis, Warren, *On Becoming A Leader*, Reading/London, Addison-Wesley/Random Century, 1989.

Bleedorn, B. D. B., *Creative Leadership for a Global Future – Studies and Speculations*, New York, Peter Lang, 1988.

Covey, Stephen R., *Principle Centred Leadership*, London/New York, Simon and Schuster, 1992.

DuBrin, Andrew J., *Leadership: Research Findings, Practice and Skills*, Boston, Houghton Mifflin Company, 1995.

Fiedler, F. E., *Improving Leadership Effectiveness, The Leader Match Concept*, New York, John Wiley, 1982.

Fiedler, F. E., *A Theory of Leadership Effectiveness*, New York, McGraw Hill, 1967.

Galbraith, J. K., *Anatomy of Power*, London, Corgi, 1985.

Handy, Charles, *Inside Organisations*, London, BBC Books, 1990.

Handy, Charles, *The Empty Raincoat*, (UK title) *The Age of Paradox* (US title), Cambridge MA/London, Harvard Business School Press, Hutchinson, 1993.

Harvey-Jones, Sir John, *Making it Happen: Reflections on Leadership*, Glasgow, Harper-Collins, 1988.

Hendry, John (ed) *et al.*, *Strategic Thinking: Leadership and the Management of Change*, Chichester, New York, John Wiley and Sons, 1993.

Hertzberg, Frederick, *Work and the Nature of Man*, London, Granada Publishing, 1971.

Katzenbach, Jon R. and Smith, Douglas, *The Wisdom of Teams Creating the High Performance Organisation*, Boston, Harvard Business School Press, 1993.

Kakabadse, A., *Working in Organizations*, London, Penguin, 1988.

Kets de Vries, Manfred F., *Prisoners of Leadership*, New York / Chichester, John Wiley and Sons, 1989.

McGregor, Douglas, *Leadership and Motivation*, Cambridge MA / London, Massachusetts Institute of Technology Press, 1966.

Mileham, Patrick, *Coming on Board, The Non-executive Director's Role in Strengthening Boardroom Leadership*, London, Institute of Management, 1995.

Normann, R., *Service Management: Strategy and Leadership in Service Business*, Chichester, John Wiley and Sons, 1991.

Peters, Tom and Austin N., *Passion for Excellence: The Leadership Difference*, Glasgow, Fontana Collins, 1985.

Schein, Edgar H., *Organisational Culture and Leadership*, 2nd edition, San Francisco, Jossey-Bass, 1992.

Syrett, Michel and Hogg, Clare (Eds), *Frontiers of Leadership*, Oxford, Basil Blackwood, 1992.

Vroom, V. H. and Jago, A. G., *The New Leadership: Managing Participation in Organizations*, Englewood Cliffs NJ, Prentice Hall, 1988.

Yukl, G. A., *Leadership in Organizations*, 3rd edition, Englewood Cliffs NJ, Prentice Hall, 1994.

INDEX